The Art of Growing Older

It's Not Age: It's Attitude and Ability

Joan Donaldson-Yarmey

Print ISBNs
Amazon print 9780228631903
Ingram Spark 9780228631910
BWL Print 9780228631927

Copyright 2025 by Joan Donaldson-Yarmey
Editor Nancy M Bell
Cover artist Pandora Designs

All rights reserved. Without limiting the rights under copyright reserved above, no part of this publication may be reproduced, stored in or introduced into a retrieval system, or transmitted, in any form, or by any means (electronic, mechanical, photocopying, recording, or otherwise) without the prior written permission of both the copyright owner and the publisher of this book.

Dedication

To
Gwen, Roy, George, Avenel, Carson, Lois.

And To
Salliann, Ron, Eli, Yvonne, Iris, Michael, and Matthew who, sadly, never made it halfway to their life's potential. To Ruth, and Syd who lived into their seventies. And to Brittany who didn't make it a quarter of the way.

Author's Note

I am not a doctor, nor do I have any medical training other than that of a caregiver. Everyone's aging journey is different and most of what is in this book is about my life and how the way I've lived it has affected my aging. The medical information I have included comes from what I have gathered from reading books, watching health shows, surfing the Internet, and listening to the latest health news (see bibliography at end). That information is always changing as new research is completed or older studies are reinterpreted. What I have written in this book should not be taken as medical advice. The opinions expressed here are solely mine as the author.

Forward

I was eighteen and in my last year of high school when Canada's Centennial celebrations were held in Montreal in 1967. I put down a deposit of $10.00 to book a place on a school-sponsored trip to those festivities. Then my boyfriend asked me to marry him, and I said yes. I cancelled my trip and began my wedding plans. The marriage lasted eight years.

Since then. I have joked that I have to live to 120 years-of-age so I could go to Canada's Bicentennial celebrations. I would be 118 in 2067 so I figured that by living to 120, I would have a couple of years to remember and talk about my experience.

Then, in 2017, Canada celebrated its 150th birthday and I turned 68 years-of-age. I was surprised that fifty years had already passed since I first made that statement. I realized that I was halfway to Canada's bicentennial.

Although it started out as a joke I have learned that it is not an unrealistic quest, that I could conceivably live to 120 years-of-age. Every year thousands of people around the world are reaching their 100th birthdays and becoming centenarians; many are even becoming super centenarians by turning 110.

Some are reaching 115 and 117 and 119 years of age. One woman has actually lived to 122 years, 164 days.

If she could do it then why couldn't others? Why couldn't I? I could think of no reason why I couldn't, so I decided to give it a try, to work at living to 120 years of age or longer.

Too bad, though, that for those first fifty years I didn't look after my body, and therefore my health, as well as I should have.

Table of Contents

Chapter 1 10
Chapter 2 26
Chapter 3 40
Chapter 4 55
Chapter 5 77
Chapter 6 83
Chapter 7 89
Chapter 8 95
Chapter 9 107
Chapter 10 117
Chapter 11 122
Chapter 12 134
Chapter 13 138
Chapter 14 148
Chapter 15 152
Chapter 16 161
Chapter 17 169
Chapter 18 186
Chapter 19 194
Chapter 20 210
Chapter 21 215

Chapter 22	232
Chapter 23	241
Chapter 24	250
Chapter 25	270
Chapter 26	286
Chapter 27	305

Part One
My Life Before Cancer

Chapter 1

My Childhood and Early Adult Life

I was born in New Westminster, B.C., Canada, part of the first wave of the Baby Boomer generation. When I was two-years-old my parents moved to a farm near Edmonton, Alberta, and a couple of years later into the city of Edmonton. Mine was a normal childhood for the time, which meant nutritious food and plenty of outdoor activity.

The house we lived in was small, but the back yard was large. There were rows of raspberries and strawberries dividing it into a lawn and a garden spot. Every summer, Mom put in a huge garden. We had fresh raspberries and strawberries when they were ripe, vegetables when they were ready, and she canned dozens of jars for over the winter. She also canned pears and peaches, which she bought from the store. There were always oranges, apples, and milk for snacks in the refrigerator. Mom made homemade white bread every week.

Every morning we had hot oatmeal for breakfast. It wasn't until I was in my teens that I was allowed to have cold packaged cereal on the weekends although my parents still ate their porridge. My siblings and I came home from school for lunch which was usually soup or salmon sandwiches or macaroni. For our suppers we ate the left over roast beef and trimmings from our Sunday meal, or canned beans and bread, scrambled eggs and toast, or pancakes and natural peanut butter. This was before the manufacturers added hydrogenated vegetable oil, salt, and sugar to the peanut butter to ensure a longer shelf life, so there was always oil on the top when we opened the lid. My dad used a butter knife to blend the oil back into the mixture before we ate it.

All our meals were homemade. We never went to restaurants and there weren't packaged or prepared frozen meals on the market. We couldn't afford any junk food or fast food that might have been available at the time. We never had chocolate bars or candy in the house except on Halloween. On that night I tried to stay out as long as possible to get as many goodies as I could. I ate everything else in my bag except the hard candy which usually lasted until Christmas because I didn't really like it.

The only downside by today's standards was that we ate strictly white bread, first homemade and then later store bought, and margarine.

Even at an early age I loved food and was a big eater. I would eat the lunch my mother prepared, then hurry over to my girlfriend's house and have lunch with her and her parents. Her mother made the best chicken noodle soup.

During grades three, four, and five, each spring all the children in the school I attended were given a three-month supply of cod liver oil capsules to take. I still remember how terrible they tasted. I used to drop the capsule in my hot porridge and stir it around so that I didn't know which mouthful I would be eating it in.

I had the usual childhood diseases, such as chicken pox, measles, and mumps and none of them were very serious. I never broke a bone nor had any serious accidents. I do remember going to visit the doctor for boils that I would get under my arms. One time he decided to lance one without giving me any painkiller or freezing it first. Even now I can feel the knife slicing through the skin and him squeezing the pus out. I was given a lotion to put on them and I eventually outgrew them.

I was a child before television, and I basically lived outside with my friends. We played games, rode our bikes, skated in the winter, and walked to school. At school we had recess, physical education, and track meets to train for. I had a very active childhood. I also got my first job at age ten.

A woman in the neighbourhood made corsages and she hired some of us children to sell them a week before Mother's Day. She would give each of us a box containing about eight corsages of different colours, and we would go to separate streets.

At each house I climbed the front stairs and knocked on the door. When it was opened I showed the different corsages and explained who had made them and how much they were worth. If a man answered, he usually bought one for his wife. If a woman answered, it was a much tougher sell. But I made enough money to buy my mother a bouquet of artificial flowers for Mother's Day.

Then we moved into a larger house in a new neighbourhood that was on the outskirts of the city. I started taking lunch to school. Bologna was cheap and for years that was what made up the majority of our lunch sandwiches. One day, my brother told Mom that he was getting tired of the same sandwich every day. But I stuck up for those sandwiches. I liked bologna. I don't know if his sandwiches changed but mine stayed basically the same until I graduated. Occasionally for variety, Mom switched tomato or cheese for the bologna.

When I turned twelve, I started earning my own money through paper delivery and babysitting and that is when my food choices really changed. A few times a week I went to a nearby restaurant for chocolate sundaes or French fries with friends after school or we'd meet on weekends. We still didn't have what today we term as junk food in the house, so I had to buy my own. I bought chocolate bars and ate two at a time. If the people I was babysitting for left a large bag of chips out for me to snack on, I would eat the whole bag. I was suddenly getting plenty of sugar and fats in my diet.

I also began bingeing at home, making myself bread and jam, or bread and cheese, sandwiches before supper. Not just one or two, but until I was full. And then I would eat supper an hour later.

Because she now worked, Fridays were the only day that Mom still made bread and that was because Dad, who worked out of town during the week, was coming home for the weekend. I sometimes bought the family a chocolate cake and chocolate swirl ice cream for dessert with our Friday night suppers.

My first real job was at a small, drive-in restaurant, which I had to walk about two kilometres to. The owner let the staff eat hamburgers, fries, milkshakes, and ice cream at a discount. My next job was in a Kentucky Fried Chicken, (KFC as it is known today), outlet which was closer to my home. There, staff could eat all the chicken we wanted. I indulged until eventually the novelty wore off.

I was still very active. I had lots of friends at our new house, and we had the freedom of biking into the countryside for exploration. Occasionally, I biked over to see my former friends and I was still walking to school.

As I advanced into junior high school there were new and varied sports introduced to our physical education. I began playing basketball, volleyball, baseball, and badminton. I even learned a few dance steps. Since I was good at sports I belonged to the school's volleyball and basketball teams. We practiced two days a week after school and travelled to other schools to play games and tournaments.

In high school I also joined the school teams. And I still walked everywhere because it was unheard of for my parents to drive me to my friend's house, or downtown, or to high school football games at other schools. Swimming and figure skating were two more activities I took in gym class.

One memory stands out very clearly from my teen years. It was to have an effect on the next four decades of my life.

When I was in grade nine one of my teachers decided that as a gracious community gesture our class would hold a spring tea for the seniors who lived in a nearby lodge. And to bridge the generation gap each of the students would "adopt" one of the seniors as an honorary grandparent.

"When your adopted grandparent arrives, he or she will be shown to their place at a table and it will be your responsibility to serve them tea and cake and to get to know them," my teacher explained.

On the day of the tea, we decorated the gymnasium with balloons and streamers and waited. Because this was such a novel idea there was a television reporter and cameraman from the local television station to cover the event. Later that evening I watched myself and some of the other students on the news.

Finally, the seniors' bus pulled up. The boys who had been assigned to help them off the bus rushed out. From just inside the gymnasium doorway, I watched the sea of white heads as the old men and women slowly made their way down the hall. The women were dressed in their best outfits with their sparse hair done up and rouge on their wrinkled cheeks. The men wore ill-fitting suits or pants and shirts. Some walked on their own, some used walkers or canes, and some were helped. This was before most places were wheelchair accessible so no one who may have been in a wheelchair attended.

I was one of the greeters and I stood at the door waiting to welcome them. As each approached I pinned a corsage on the women's dresses and the men's shirts or suit coats. Most of them smiled or said thank you but a few looked lost as if they weren't sure where they were or what they were doing here. Once they had their corsage they were escorted to their tables, which were set so that there would be two "grandparents" and two "grandchildren" at each one.

When everyone was seated I went to the long table holding the pieces of cake and picked up two plates. I carried them to the table where my "grandmother" sat and introduced myself.

"What do you take in your tea?" I asked.

"Just a little sugar," she said, her voice shaky.

I went to the tea pots and poured her a cup. I didn't drink tea so grabbed a glass of juice and returned to our table. I had a difficult time relating to my adopted grandmother. Conversation was hard. Three of my natural grandparents died before I knew them. I don't ever remember doing anything one-on-one with the grandmother who was part of my life. She was always at family gatherings but as a child I don't recall us ever spending a day or even an afternoon together.

I looked around the room. While most of the seniors seemed happy with the tea, I felt pity for them. I didn't like the idea that they needed to be adopted, like a stray cat or dog, or someone no one else wanted. I felt sorry that they were old.

As I walked home after school I thought about the afternoon. I knew that I never wanted to be in the position where I had to have strangers "adopt" me. I never wanted to be old.

And that was when, at the age of fifteen, I decided that I would commit suicide when I reached sixty-five years of age. I would not go through those years of my life as a lonely, old woman waiting for someone to be nice to me.

* * *

I met my first husband while working at KFC. He'd been raised on a farm northeast of Edmonton but was now employed by his brother in the service station next door. We began dating during the winter and he told me he was only working for his brother temporarily and that someday he wanted to return to his childhood farm and become a farmer. He took me out to the farm to meet his parents where I was introduced to feeding and watering the cows and pigs, gathering eggs from the chickens, and haying, all of which was a novelty to me. But I never got to really see what day to day farm life was like. We became engaged in the spring and his father told him that he wanted to retire from farming. They worked out a deal where my future husband would use the equipment and do the farming and give his parents a percentage of the income. He moved to the farm and began preparing for spring seeding.

We married one month after I graduated high school and I moved from the city to the farm. Thus began a tough time in my life. My life was totally transformed. I was lifted out of my secure, comfortable, active existence and dropped into a totally different, foreign way of living. It's not that I didn't know it was going to happen. It's just that I hadn't foreseen what it would be like to live there permanently; that it was going to be my total life every day, and that I could not step back into my former life whenever I wanted, like I had stepped back after a weekend visit.

We built a small house in the same yard as his parents, both of whom worked in town. After living in the city with its conveniences, I had no indoor plumbing, which meant no running water or toilet. I had to carry water from the well for drinking and from my in-laws' house to wash clothes. Before my marriage and move I hadn't needed a driver's licence because I walked to most places I wanted to go or took a city bus. Now, if I wanted to go shopping I had to wait until my husband had the time.

The hardest part was going from having friends, working, and earning my own money, and being very socially active, to living on a quiet farm, knowing no one in the community, not having a way of getting anywhere, and really, having nowhere to go.

My husband spent the summer in the fields. I helped out when it was something I could handle like cultivating the summer fallow.

No one knew about stress at that time and how it can affect our bodies. Looking back, I can see that I was under a lot of stress during that first year. It took a lot of mental and emotional strength on my part to adjust to not having any family or friends living nearby; to losing the freedom I had to go wherever I wanted when I wanted; to not having much money after earning my own money since the age of twelve; to spending my days alone after the hectic life of high school. The first year I had no radio, which meant no music, no news, no noise.

When my husband got a job for the winter I was alone in the house. My days became ones of total silence. There weren't any birds to sing, any dogs to bark, nor did any vehicles drive by. We had no telephone so I couldn't even call anyone. Total silence. Total solitude.

Time slowed down. There was no mad rushing to get ready for school, to go to work, to prepare for the next party. There was no schedule to keep and the only one to talk to was me. I really got to know myself and to understand myself. I developed a very good relationship with myself. I became my best friend and confidant.

Then my mother-in-law leant me a record player and a few records. They weren't the Beatles or Dave Clark Five or the Mamas and Papas, but I listened to them all day until I had every song memorized. Today, there is one song, *Still* by Bill Anderson, that I can sing all the words to.

I knew nothing about farming. One day my in-laws, my husband, and I were discussing buying baby chicks to raise for meat and to supply us with eggs. They came in three different types: those that would eventually become hens, which cost the most; those that would become roosters, which cost the least; and unsexed which were priced in between.

"How do you unsex a chick," I asked, picturing a person with tweezers or some elaborate machine.

When the laughter died down they explained to me that "unsexed" meant that the chicks had not been sorted into females and males.

In the spring my parents gave us a radio, and in the fall, my father-in-law found us a used black and white television. I was finally able to keep up with what was happening in the rest of the world. However, it was during that first year that I realized the only person I could totally depend on was me.

Over the next several years I did get to know our neighbours and made lots of friends. We had two children and developed a social life. I got my driver's licence, joined a baseball team in the summer, and played volleyball and basketball in the winter.

I slowly grew to like living in the country although I always felt that my life was passing without me accomplishing anything, that I was missing out on a lot of living, especially when I'd return to the city for a visit. There my friends had jobs, were travelling the world, had excitement in their lives. And since I had always thought that the best part of my life would basically be over by the time I reached forty, I was worried. All I had to look forward to for the rest of my life was planting my garden in the spring, weeding it during the summer, and harvesting the vegetables in the fall.

We eventually bought the farm and moved into the bigger house. However, farm life was not the easiest. Our finances were never very good; prices of beef and pork and grain fluctuated so that we seldom made more than it cost us to operate. We had three quarters of a section of land, and we bought two more hoping the increase in grain production would help out. But it never did so my husband, who would not concede that farming was a futile endeavour, continued to work during the winters to keep us afloat.

For the most part our eating was good. Every summer we had fresh vegetables from my garden, and I froze them for the winter. I raised chickens for meat and eggs. We also butchered our own steers and pigs. Our cattle ate grass during the summer and hay or silage in the winter. Our pigs were fed grain, which we harvested from our land. While there were no growth hormones or other additives in the feed, my husband did use fertilizer and spray on our crops.

The beef was cut into large steaks, roasts, stew meat, and made into hamburger. I can remember the thick pork chops from the pigs that were liberally trimmed with fat. I fried them up and we would have a full meal of mashed potatoes, meat, and vegetables. I would cut a portion of the pork chop, making sure there was a piece of fat attached. The taste was so good.

My husband went hunting in the fall and we had wild meat to give variety to our meals. He also occasionally went fishing in a nearby lake.

We couldn't afford much more than the basics in food. We never bought pop or snack foods like chips. I remember going to visit friends who could afford these. I envied them and ate and drank as much as I could while we played cards.

Neither did we have store-bought pastries in the house. To make up for it, though, I became an excellent baker and the overeating I had begun in my teen years continued. I made cakes, cookies, and pies which were high in lard or hydrogenated margarine, sugars, and white flour. Also, when times were tough we ate bologna in sandwiches, or fried with eggs for breakfast.

But I wanted more for my life. I mentioned to my husband that maybe I should get a job in town to help with the finances. I thought that it would get me out with people, and I would be earning some money. He replied, "No wife of mine is going to work."

With the extra farmland my husband hired a man to help with the field work in the summer. I suggested that we hire a babysitter instead and I would assist in the field. I just needed to be doing something. But again, he refused to consider the idea.

To keep busy during the winter I learned to knit and crochet and then I began making petite point jewellery which was very popular at the time. I would take it to the Farmer's Market and sell it. I also took up painting and I tried some writing, which when I look back, was quite bad.

However, after eight years of each of us trying to deal with our differing desires, we separated and eventually divorced.

Then I married again and began a blended family. We had my children most of the time with my step-children coming for holidays or moving in with us for a while. It was hard on everyone because the children had to deal with different rules than they were used to. And while our children were in the same age group, they didn't always get along. We parents didn't always concur on discipline or were in agreement with our step-children. At one point I told my step-daughter, "We are both learning. You have never had a step-mother and I have never had a step-daughter. I don't know how to act or do things any more than you do."

Those years were harder on some of us than on others, but we all did the best we knew how at the time. I am proud to say that

I have a strong relationship with my biological children, and also with my step-children who call me Mom. When people ask me how many children I have I say five, two daughters and three sons. Unfortunately, my two step-sons have died.

Chapter 2

My Forties and Early Fifties

I raised my children when I was in my twenties and thirties and worked at various jobs. Then in my mid-thirties I took some writing courses. I sent out articles and short stories to magazines but only received back rejection letters. We lived on an acreage at the time and had to go into the nearest town for our mail. One day my son who, with his girlfriend had stopped in to check the mail on their way to school, drove back into the yard and came into the house. He handed me a letter.

"I saw it was from a publisher and thought you might want it," he said.

I opened it thinking it was just another rejection but inside was an acceptance letter for a personal story I had written and a cheque for one hundred dollars. I was so amazed and thrilled that I began jumping around the room hugging everyone two or three times. I had finally done it.

My son's girlfriend stayed out in the truck and later she told me that she had asked him what happened. He explained that I had made my first sale.

"Was she excited?" she asked.

"She must have been," he replied. "She was swearing."

The guest speaker at one of my writing courses was the publisher of a small, non-fiction publishing company in Edmonton. He gave a great talk encouraging us to write, write, write. During the question section, I mentioned that one manuscript I had sent away had come back rejected but with a letter that said it had taken two readings before it was decided the novel wasn't for them. He told me I should rewrite it and send it out again. But I had come up with another idea for my writing. I was almost forty years of age and in need of making a mark in my life.

Alberta at the time was divided into tourist zones. I thought that a book describing each zone and its particular attractions might have merit, so I sent a proposal to that publisher soon after the course. He wrote back that it was worth looking at and I made an appointment to visit him. However, we had differing ideas on the content of the books. I wanted to describe the towns and the sights of each zone while he wanted to get into the historical and cultural side. And we could not come to an agreement.

When I stood up to leave, I said. "Well, if nothing else, while I am working on my idea

I will at least see all the back roads of Alberta."

"I've always wanted to do a book on the back roads of Alberta," he said.

I sat back down, and we discussed the project. It would be a big undertaking. I would have to drive all the roads in the whole province. I wasn't sure how long it would take to do that and then bring everything together into a book. At the end he said. "If you can write it, I will publish it."

As I approached the big 40 I was in awe that I didn't feel any different than I had when I turned twenty or thirty. My perception of who I would be at that age had been wrong. I wasn't old and about to enter my senior hood. My life was good. Sixty-five was still a long ways off and I had a book to work on, something I'd been wanting for years.

So, I planned a huge party for my 40th birthday. I invited family and friends and told them it was to take place over the weekend and to come when they could. I went to the secondhand store and found a dress, shoes, stockings, hat, and purse and for both Friday and Saturday nights I dressed as the little old lady I had, since childhood pictured I would be. I walked slowly and stooped over and talked in a scratchy voice. But I couldn't maintain it for very long. I quickly changed into my regular clothes again. I didn't even want to pretend I was old.

It took a total of two years for me to do the travelling and the writing for my book. I spent about two months during the summer driving the roads in my four-wheel drive vehicle with my cockapoo dog. We camped wherever we found a spot when it was too dark to take pictures and were up as soon as it was light enough to take pictures. Then it was arranging all that I had learned into a book.

I sent it to the publisher and in the process of them doing the layout it was decided to divide it into two books: *Backroads of Northern Alberta* and *Backroads of Southern Alberta*. They were scheduled to be released in the fall of 1992.

In the spring of 1992, my husband, Mike, and I were preparing for both a death and a wedding in our family. At the beginning of that year, Mike's oldest sister, Salliann, had been diagnosed with terminal pancreatic cancer, and my son and his fiancé had set a wedding date. Salliann had always maintained a good weight, but she smoked. For almost five months we visited her, first at home and then in the hospital. I cannot describe the anger, sorrow, and frustration I felt as I watched what the disease was doing to her. She lost weight and the ability to look after herself.

For those same five months I experienced a mother's delight and happiness as I helped with the wedding plans. I made the cake, found my dress, arranged for my hairdo, and organized a mixed shower of friends and family. I was also working and excited about my first books being published.

Balancing my life while dealing with all the emotions was truly difficult. When finally confined to hospital, Salliann lived for many weeks. I worked the evening shift at my job and sometimes after getting off work at one o'clock in the morning I would go and just sit in the hospital room watching her sleep. During her final month she was hardly more than a skeleton.

Then one evening I was called at work and told that she was being given Last Rites by her priest. I hurried to the hospital and joined the rest of the family gathered around her bed. But she didn't die as expected. In fact, within a couple of days she was able to be wheeled outside the hospital so she could have a cigarette. Apparently, her body wasn't ready to give up.

Salliann died at age fifty-four and four weeks later over 300 friends and relatives attended my son's wedding and partied well into the night. Like most people it took a death to make Mike and I realize how important *really living* was. We knew we had to do something adventurous with our lives, something out of the ordinary. So that fall we quit our jobs, sold our house, and went to stake a gold claim in southern British Columbia.

We returned to Edmonton so I could do interviews and book signings when my books were published then spent the winter in our holiday trailer in a campground in Vancouver. In the spring we headed to the claim. Over the spring and summer, we explored the area, panned for gold, watched deer walk through our camp, listened to birds singing and rain drops falling on our roof, and generally enjoyed our break from life.

By the summer's end our sojourn was over. We never did find much gold but then it really wasn't about the gold.

When we got back to Edmonton I phoned a woman I'd become friends with at the place where I'd worked to let her know I was back and looking for a job. Two hours later the manager phoned and asked if I could start the next day. Mike also got a job, and we settled back into the real world again.

Within a year I was laid off. I had another chat with my publisher, and I spent the next four years travelling and camping through British Columbia with my dog. I had a larger truck and a camperette for those trips. I researched and wrote four back roads books for that province. I was a little more organized, so it didn't take as long to do the research and writing. Then I headed north to the Yukon and Alaska for a combined book on them. I traded my dog for my husband on that excursion because we both loved the Yukon.

But life never runs smoothly. In 1998, Mike's brother, Eli, passed away at age fifty-seven from cancer. And then in 1999, we lost Mike's mom, Pauline, to a heart attack.

* * *

A week before my fiftieth birthday I got a tattoo on the outside of my left ankle. It is a red heart with a red 50 inside. The tattoo artist was considerate and although it hurt, it wasn't as bad as I had expected. I joked and told him that I would like him to do my next tattoo which would also be a red heart but with a 100 inside for my hundredth birthday on my right ankle. He said that if he was still doing tattoos at the time, he would.

Again, I discovered that my perception of fifty was inaccurate. I was not physically and mentally dysfunctional as I had originally imagined. I was still the same me. There was no line that I stepped across which took me from being young to being old. Some senile, elderly person did not suddenly take over my mind, and my body did not become frail and decrepit.

I planned another birthday party. This time, though, I dressed as a hooker/biker chick. I wore a short red skirt, leather jacket with chains hanging on it, black fishnet stockings, and spike heels. I donned a cheap artificial red wig and carried a whip.

My life was still good. I had changed my writing style and was trying to break into the fiction market.

But life quickly changed. In the early summer of 2000 I noticed that my father seemed pale and slower in his walking. He'd had arthritis in his back for many years and it had been getting worse. In August of that year Mom and Dad invited my siblings and I and our spouses over for a family supper. For some reason I was scared, and I said to Mike. "There's something wrong with Dad."

After the meal dad left the table to go sit in his chair and watch TV. Mom then said. "Your dad has prostate cancer, and it has spread to other organs and to his bones. There is nothing that can be done."

We all sat in silence for a few moments. "You mean its terminal?" I asked.

"Yes," Mom answered.

Thus began a flurry of visits from family and friends. I spent time going to the doctor and the cancer clinic with my parents. One of Dad's legs was swollen, and Mom would rub it to give him some relief from the pain. Then one morning I received a phone call from Mom that Dad had collapsed and she had called 911. She gave me the name of the hospital they were going to. I told Mike and quickly went there. He phoned the rest of the family to let them know.

Dad was on morphine and drifted in and out of consciousness. Tests were run and it was found that his heart wasn't beating normally. While we were waiting for a person to administer an electric shock to settle the rhythm of his heart, the doctor asked Mom if they should resuscitate Dad if the shock caused his heart to stop beating. Mom looked at me for help. I could not answer. She said yes.

I thought back to when I was a child, and I told my mother that I wanted to be the first to die in our family so that I would not have to go through the sadness of losing someone.

"What about our feelings if you die?" she'd asked.

As a child that was something I hadn't thought about and as I waited with my mother in the hospital, I didn't care about. It was my pain that was important. I did not want to lose my father.

It only took one treatment and Dad's heart settled into its natural rhythm. The doctor decided that because of the circumstances, Dad should be kept in the hospital for a few days. We went to visit him the next day and he was still drifting on the morphine. In the middle of that night Mom phoned to say that she had received a call from the hospital that Dad had died—a clot had gone from his leg to his heart. Mike and I rushed over to pick her up and we drove to the hospital to say goodbye. It was three weeks from the day we had learned the news.

In January of 2001 I discovered a lump in my right breast. It was a month until my scheduled mammogram, but I phoned the centre I went to for my yearly check-ups and told the receptionist what I had found. She immediately set up an appointment for me in two days. I had had a benign tumour removed from my left breast when I was forty and benign calcium deposits taken from that same area when I was forty-five. This time I strongly suspected, even before I went into the appointment, that I had cancer.

As soon as I arrived I was ushered into the nurse's office. Right from the first question, does it hurt? I sensed I was right, since "No." was my answer. The second indication was that after the mammogram I was taken in for an ultrasound. No one said the word "cancer", but I was then asked to undergo a biopsy. The technologist said that it usually took a few days to schedule but she could do it right then if I wanted. The actual confirmation for me came when I was told by my doctor that I should bring other members of my family to hear the results of the biopsy in a few days.

I had been expecting it. I take after my father's side of the family and three of his sisters had had breast cancer. One died in her fifties while the other two had both breasts removed. Of them, one lived to be ninety-two years old and the other eighty-five.

The lump was 2 cm in diameter and was stage two cancer. Because of that and my age I was told I should have a lumpectomy, then chemotherapy and radiation. I was given a choice of the type of chemotherapy treatment, and I opted for one which was not as strong but involved six injections and then pills for three weeks after each injection.

The first treatment did not make me physically ill, but very nauseous. I tried anti-nausea pills, but they only made the feeling worse. Before the second injection I had to have my white blood count taken. Normally it is around seven but mine was 0.5. I had to wait a week and have it tested again. It was over 4.5, so I had my next round of chemo. By the end of the three weeks of pills, my esophagus and stomach would be on fire. I ate a lot of ice cream trying to put the flames out.

This was my routine for over six months.o

During the week that I had to wait for my white blood count to increase, I had to stay away from people so as not to catch any infections, but it was also the week I would start to feel better. Sometimes it took a lot of courage to go back to the clinic knowing I was sentencing myself to three more weeks of illness.

But I consider myself one of the lucky ones. I was only in the chemotherapy treatment room for about an hour. Some people were there for three hours. Others, who had a full day session, were put in bed and usually vomited during their treatment.

While I was on chemo, we received a phone call that Mike's dad, Yaris, had suffered a stroke and was in the hospital. We rushed to see him. He couldn't speak but he did recognize us. We watched him slowly deteriorate over a few days then die. His funeral was on his eighty-seventh birthday.

My radiation lasted five weeks. I found my lump in mid-January, and it was removed February 12. My last radiation treatment was in December. Almost a year of my life but then again, only a year of my life. I have been cancer free since.

I do not now, nor ever did, consider my cancer life-threatening. I would rather have had my year of cancer and treatment and be over with it then have a chronic illness such as Crohn's Disease or Fibromyalgia, which many people I know have. Both of those last a lifetime. Nor do I want to be defined by the disease. I don't introduce myself as Joan, breast cancer survivor. In fact, it seldom comes up in my conversations. I would rather talk about my family, my writing, my holiday plans, or what I want to do next week.

A few days before my surgery I had to go into the hospital to meet with my surgeon and anesthesiologist to learn how the procedure would go. I also met with a woman from the cancer society. She told me about a support group that I could join. They would meet once a month and over coffee and lunch, share their problems, joys, and fears about dealing with cancer. I knew that wasn't for me. But maybe there was something else that would be.

A couple of years before, I had seen a news item about a dragon boat team made up of breast cancer survivors who had taken part in the dragon boat festival in Vancouver, British Columbia. As I watched the show I thought that dragon boating looked like fun and that I would like to do it someday. I guess it's a case of, *Be careful what you wish for*.

I asked the woman if there was a breast cancer survivor dragon boat team in Edmonton. She said yes and gave me a contact name.

Two weeks after my surgery I went down to watch them train which, because it was winter, took place in a swimming pool. I gave the treasurer a cheque and joined the Breast Friends Dragon Boat team. They have a policy that a new member can't take part in any training or practice sessions until three months after her last chemo or radiation treatment. Although I couldn't be an active member until the following year, I did attend meetings which were held every month. Besides the regular business someone usually had an update on something new in the cancer world.

One meeting was about to reshape my future. One of the ladies mentioned that she had read that sugar can cause cancer and that cancer loves sugar and actually thrived on the sugar we consume. I looked down at the can of cola I was drinking and thought about all the colas I had drank and chocolate bars and other sweets I had eaten during my lifetime and even during my treatment.

It dawned on me how little I knew about what contributed to the health of my body. And since my health had suddenly become very important to me I decided it was time I learned all I could about it. That learning process has been ongoing as new studies are done and new articles and books are published.

Chapter 3
My Lifelong Love Affair With Eating and the Nutrition in My Foods

I had always known that a *proper* diet was important to a healthy body. I knew that vegetables and fruits were better for me than chocolate cake but that wasn't enough to make me decline the cake and reach for the celery. The books I read taught me why a diet was so important. They explained how harmful so much of the food I have eaten in the past has been to my body's cells and systems and therefore to my health. And some of it frightened me because for much of my life food has been my addiction of choice.

I eat when I am happy, I eat when I am sad, I eat when I am stressed, but mostly, I eat for the pure enjoyment of it. Having a full stomach is security for me. And I don't know why. There was always food on the table when I was growing up. I was never abused. I don't have any deep dark, hidden memory of a terrible incident. It is a plain and simple fact that I love food. I love eating and for most of my first seventy-five plus years I didn't just eat until I was full, I ate until I was stuffed. If it tasted really good I ate to the point of sickness.

There is that saying, "Everything is okay in moderation", but I didn't know the meaning of that word. It's not that I didn't always eat beneficial foods, it's that I usually ate a lot of the bad foods. And maybe it could be called a habit since I've always overeaten. It is the only way I knew how to eat.

Throughout my childhood and teen years, I ate what was in my parent's house. If I wanted something else, like chocolate bars, I would have to buy them myself. But when I became a wife and mother, food became my priority. I had to shop for it, cook it, and serve it. I had to make sure there was something for breakfast, lunches, supper, and snacks. It was under my domain what was in the house and what was served for meals—fruit, vegetables, bread, meats, and desserts. But that also made food my life. It took up a lot of my thoughts, my time. Even when I worked, food was still my responsibility.

During my second marriage I have lived on acreages, in small towns, and in cities. We have a combined family and as the children were growing, I really put my cooking and baking skills to work. I still overate and I also began drinking cola.

I put in a garden, but it was usually small and yielded only enough for us to eat during the summer. There were never any vegetables to freeze.

Once my children were grown up and gone, I would like to say that food lost its priority, but it didn't. It remained a large part of my life for many years. Since there weren't as many eaters in the house I went from baking my desserts to buying them.

I have binged on so many different foods throughout my adulthood. Whenever I found a dessert I liked, I would make it over and over again. If I was at someone's house and they served something new I made sure to get the recipe before I left. Then I would put it into my repertoire of main courses or desserts that I made every day. Sometimes, I would binge on the food for weeks at a time. Even when I tried to stop, the urge became so overpowering that it took over my mind and didn't let go until I ate it. It wasn't until my mind and body became saturated and did not crave it anymore that I could quit. This might take a month or longer.

When I began shopping for my binge foods, if I liked it I would buy it over and over again. But it wasn't just desserts that I ate. I liked my meats and potatoes and breads, and I am embarrassed to admit that I could out eat many men I sat down with at the table.

Some of my binges were short term, but most of them lasted months or even years. And they were just part of the eating I did each day. I still ate my regular meals.

The following is just a fraction of the list of my binges over my lifetime:

While on the farm I went through a spell of eating cornflakes with fresh cream and brown sugar. It was so good but eventually I tired of the heavy cream and have never done it again.

I would bake four dozen chocolate chip cookies at a time. I would leave two dozen out for the family and freeze the rest. In short order I would eat the first ones and I found that when I had the craving and there were none thawed, even frozen ones tasted good.

I picked wild fruit in the fall and made jams and jellies. My favourite was pin cherry jelly. When I made bread, I would cut a piece of bread, slather it with margarine, and top that with pin cherry jelly. I could eat three-quarters of a loaf of bread and a jar of jelly this way in one sitting.

Hard margarine (the trans-fats in it weren't known at the time) was the cheapest to buy and was what we ate. I love peanut butter sandwiches. To make them I would take two slices of white bread and spread margarine on both of them. Then I would heap on the peanut butter which was full of hydrogenated vegetable oil, sugar and salt. I could consume two or three in a sitting.

I like chocolate sundaes with whipped cream, and they have been a staple of my bingeing over the years. When I got the craving for a chocolate sundae it usually wouldn't go away until it was satisfied. On the farm, though, we didn't always have the money, so there were times when I would have to suffer through it. However, when we had money I would phone a neighbour at work and ask him to buy me my ingredients on his way home. I did this, not once, but many, many times. Poor man. Later in my life, when our finances were better ice cream, chocolate syrup, and whipped cream were always on my grocery list.

In the fall when I took off the garden I would make carrot cake with cream cheese icing. But I never iced the cake. Instead, I would take a piece of cake, dollop a large spoonful of icing on it, and then eat it. I kept doing this through three-quarters of the cake. I liked the icing more than the cake. Once I made a cake with icing to take to a woman as a thank-you gift. I sat and ate half the cake before I left.

I got turned on to chocolate covered peanut butter balls and the love affair lasted about four years. When I first began buying them there was 320gms (11.3 oz) in a package. I could eat almost the full amount of them before my stomach would yell 'time out.' I went through bags of them this way. Then one day I found that I could eat the total pouch before my stomach protested. At first I thought my stomach had finally adjusted to the repeated assault of the chocolates, but when I checked the weight I discovered that there were now 280gms (9.9 oz) in the bag. I am not proud of the way I figured out that the manufacturer had reduced the amount of chocolates in their package without changing the size of the package.

And I had many other bad eating habits. Every day for over thirty-five years I drank at least two cans, and sometimes more, of cola.

I ate whole packages of store bought cookies in one sitting. And not just once or twice a year. I could do it for days on end, get tired of them and quit for a couple of weeks and go at it again. I always joked that the last few cookies had gone bad because I was okay up until eating them and then I would feel sick to my stomach.

While on the farm I ate bacon and eggs for most of my breakfasts. Since then, I have fried them up for any meal.

When the family celebrated birthdays or anniversaries I asked for a corner piece of cake because it had the most icing. Others would scrape off their icing and give it to me.

I would make a salad with fresh fruit– peaches, plums, pears, etc. Then I would sprinkle on lots of sugar and let it sit for a while. I explained away the sugar by saying that at least I was eating fruit. Sometimes I would use this fruit mixture as a topping for ice cream.

As Halloween neared and boxes of the small chocolate bars appeared on the store shelves, I would buy a box just to make sure I had some. But soon they would be calling my name, and I would eat them. So, I'd buy another box and the same thing would happen. Usually in the month preceding Halloween, I'd eat at least three, sometimes more, of those large boxes.

For most of my writing career I could stay at the computer longer and write better if my stomach was full and my mind not side-tracked by thoughts of food. And the best food to fill it with was chocolates.

When I didn't have any desserts in the house and I didn't feel like making any, I would take two to four slices of white bread and tear them into pieces into a bowl. I'd add milk and then liberally top the bread with corn syrup. Or for variety I would toast four pieces of bread and put on margarine. I would pour a large amount of corn syrup onto the plate and spoon it onto bits of the toast and eat them. If I ran out of syrup too soon I would add more and if I didn't have enough toast I would make more.

For a month before Christmas my alcoholic drink of choice most evenings was Kahlua with cream and milk. I usually drank them up until New Years and sometimes long afterwards.

Also, the Christmas season was a good reason to buy and eat large bags of chocolates and boxes of liqueur-filled chocolates.

I can say that I did have some good eating habits. For most of my years I have eaten fresh vegetables from my garden in the summer. These, I find, are so much better tasting than the ones bought from the store.

There were times when I decided I had to eat better so I bought vegetables and made salads. However, these periods didn't last very long, certainly not as long as my binges. One of my excuses for not making salads often was that it takes too long to cut up the vegetables and also to chew it.

For a while I made my own yogurt and sprouted alfalfa and mung bean seeds. But, again, nothing good I did endured.

I took vitamins off and on. I read *Prevention* magazine for a while and cooked and ate as they advised, but that soon petered out.

When my children were teenagers, I tried to bake wholesome foods. I used unbleached flour in my home-made bread and added cracked wheat or cornmeal to it.

When we had three teenage boys and one pre-teen girl living with us I had to do a lot of cooking and baking. I thought I was feeding them well when I put whole wheat flour in the chocolate cakes I made. I would bake two at a time and cover them with lots of chocolate icing. After school we—yes I ate too—would sit down and consume a full cake.

When I made pancakes for breakfast, I would use whole wheat flour instead of white flour.

In an effort to get my children to eat better I made their school sandwiches with one slice of white bread and one slice of whole wheat bread. I don't know to this day if they ate them, or traded them, or threw them away. No one complained though. I also put an apple in their lunches hoping they would eat it. I think most of them got tossed.

When the low fat craze first came out, like everyone else I thought low fat meant low calories. I bought low fat cookies thinking of the good I was doing my body. Then one day I compared calories and found that the numbers were basically the same. Low fat had been replaced with higher sugar which in its own way was wrecking my body.

I did try to do right. Evenings were my time to overeat. So, I tried a variety of different distractions. I did crafts such as needle point, knitting, crocheting, painting; I took evening courses; I walked to get out of the house. But when I finished my task or had completed my walk, I am still appalled at how quickly I could devour 1000 calories worth of cookies, chocolates, or ice cream.

Many times, I vowed to change my eating by cutting out the wrong foods and eating more right ones. Usually that was when I had just finished making myself ill from consuming a huge chocolate sundae, or half a cake, or most of a pie. I would be into my bingeing hangover, with its accompanying sick stomach, sluggish-feeling body, and disorganized mind. It was always easiest to commit to a diet plan on an over-full belly.

The next day I would try to remember how nauseated I felt after gorging myself as I chewed on my vegetables. But my memory always failed me and within a couple of days or maybe a week I'd be back into the high fat, high sugar, high calorie foods of my old eating habits.

Often I went from the stress of depriving myself, to the relief of eating my favourite food, to the guilt of having succumbed to the temptation. I always found that it was so much easier to plan to do right when I had a full belly and so hard to do right when I was hungry or craving something.

No one likes to deprive themselves, me most of all.

* * *

Many health practitioners believe that premature aging is caused by poor nutrition. In today's society many of us consume 59 to 68 kg (130 to 150 lbs.) of sugar a year and up to five times the amount of salt our bodies require. Our diet also contains about 40% fat. The high incidence of arthritis, osteoporosis, heart disease, stroke, and cancer that our society is experiencing at all ages only started in the last half of the twentieth century with easy access to sugar, fat, and salt-laden foods.

My past eating habits will be a huge element in my ability to live to 120 years-of-age. I cringe when I realize what I have eaten and how my body has reacted to it. I can't believe that I so willingly abused my body for the sake of taste.

I found an abundance of different advice, though, on what are the best foods to eat and when and how. Some research advocates high protein low carbohydrates, others a high carbohydrate, low protein diet. Still more advised that I should: stay away from dairy; eat more grains and nuts; don't eat meat; don't eat proteins and carbohydrates together or they will clog my system; eat protein with my carbohydrates to keep my insulin levels down; and the list goes on and on. It is almost impossible to decide which is best, and that is probably why most people just eat what they like, when they like, whether it is considered good for them or not.

Nutrients are substances that I require to build, maintain, and repair my body. They are obtained from the foods I eat, like grains, proteins, and a wide variety of brightly coloured fruits and vegetables. While my body can convert some nutrients from one form to another, such as sugar to fat, there are others it cannot. Those are termed "essential" nutrients because it is essential that I get them from the food I eat. Basically, they are the protein, carbohydrates, fats, minerals, vitamins, and water that I consume every day.

In order for my body to perform its many functions at all times of my life it needs to get nutrients from outside sources or from existing tissues. But I'm not sure if I can really get the nutrients from today's foods that my body needs.

The topsoil of the planet consists of dust, tiny chips of rock, and humus made from decomposed vegetation and animal waste. In this topsoil are bacteria, fungi, insects, and earthworms which feed on the decaying plants left from the previous year. They also aerate the soil.

For centuries farmers rotated crops letting the soil rest a year, and they used organic material to replenish the nutrients taken out the past year. When small farms gave way to larger ones, crop rotation ceased, and artificial fertilizers came into use. Much of the nourishment in the soil was lost as were the organisms that lived there. They could not survive in the acidic environment created by the nitrogen, phosphorous, and potash in the fertilizer.

Today, some of the goodness of plants grown on these poorly-managed, over-used, over-fertilized farmland soils is not as high as it once was due to the fact that the plants are not always able to find the nutrients they need in the soil. Because of this, the fruits and vegetables do not always have the nourishment that I need or expect when I eat them.

Vegetables and fruits begin to lose vitamins right after picking so how good they are depends on how long it takes to get them to the grocery shelf, how long they sit there before I purchase them, and how long they are in my fridge before I consume them.

Some authors said frozen vegetables are better than fresh ones because they are frozen soon after picking so have many of their nutrients intact. Others stated that's not true because many of the healthful aspects are lost in the blanching and freezing.

There are two types of protein: the type I get from my food, and that which is in my body. I must have protein in my diet in order to obtain the eight "essential" amino acids that my body cannot manufacture from other foods.

When I eat dietary protein my body rearranges the amino acids into the type of protein it wants. This new body protein is used to build my muscles, blood, hair, skin, nails, and to nourish my organs such as my heart and brain. The protein in meat, eggs, poultry, and milk is easily incorporated by my body because of its similarity to my own protein. These, though, contain saturated fats.

Protein is also found in soy, fish, nuts, legumes, beans, and vegetables. These foods don't contain the saturated fats found in meats, but nuts, legumes and beans need to be combined with brown rice, wheat, or barley to make healthier proteins.

Excessive consumption of protein could put a strain on my digestive and elimination systems, and may burden my kidneys, reduce my immunity, increase my cholesterol levels, cause hardening of my arteries, and lower my absorption of calcium while leaching it from my bones. There is also an increased chance that I may develop colon cancer.

I don't eat much meat but when I do I like it well done. I have learned that overcooking my protein can kill protease, the enzyme that breaks down meat into its individual amino acids. When meat becomes tough from too much heat over a long period of time, it is harder for my system to digest and to force the release of the amino acids I need. When the protein is not digested properly, the chunks could cause a buildup of acid in my system throwing my pH out of balance.

One researcher stated he believed that eating half a kilogram (1lb) of char broiled steak was equivalent to smoking 300 cigarettes in the amount of cancer causing agents it had.

I have thought about becoming a vegetarian because studies have shown that people on plant-based diets live longer, are healthier, and have a lower risk for some cancers. Also, many doctors claim that their vegetarian patients recover from illness or surgery faster than their non-vegetarian clients.

Vegetarianism is a plant-based diet that excludes all animal flesh, including poultry, seafood, and meat by-products. There are several different degrees of vegetarianism. People who are ovo-vegetarians include eggs as part of their diet; those who are lacto-ovo allow dairy products and eggs, while lacto eat dairy in their diet.

Vegans eliminate the use of dairy and eggs but also don't consume honey, or use anything made from wool, hair, silk, or feathers.

Some people believe a vegetarian diet is better for them since meat (not including fish) is a drag on the human system and is supposed to contribute to the aging process.

I have cut back on my red meats, but I feel I still need them once or twice a week to keep my iron levels up in my blood. I do eat mostly chicken, fish, and eggs, and I like my dairy products, again for the calcium they give me.

Chapter 4
Sugar and Fats

I love anything sweet, especially if chocolate is involved. All my life I have considered sugar as one of my food groups— I just wish that statement was a joke. Whether it was brown sugar on my oatmeal, toast and jam, chocolate bars, dessert after my meal, or sodas I needed my sugar fix every day. After reading about what sugar and its many pseudonyms can do to my body I am sickened to think of the damage I may have done to myself for most of my life.

I used to buy corn syrup and pour it over my bread and milk as a dessert or spread it on my toast for breakfast. High fructose corn syrup, HFCS, is a sugar substitute found in sodas, salad dressings, and many other sweet tasting foods. It was first developed in 1957 then was refined in the 1970s before it was introduced into foods. It is produced by milling corn into corn starch and then processing that to make corn syrup. This is almost entirely glucose. Enzymes are added to change the glucose into fructose. The resulting high fructose corn syrup is 90%

fructose and 10% glucose which means it is all sugars.

Just because it is called fructose, making it sound like it is from fruit, it isn't, and it isn't healthier than sugar.

Two hormones, ghrelin and leptin, control hunger and appetite. Ghrelin lets me know that my stomach is empty and needs food. Leptin, on the other hand, goes to my brain to tell it that my stomach is full. High fructose corn syrup inhibits my secretion of leptin. So, my brain doesn't always get the message that I am full. This can lead to overeating and in most cases, weight gain.

Up until the manufacture of HFCS, the sugar consumed came mainly from sugar beets or sugar cane. Since the 1970s HFCS has been added to everything from jams to soft drinks to canned goods to some health foods. Many doctors and researchers believe that the obesity crisis began with its introduction along with the removal of physical education from schools.

Every plant-based food is basically a carbohydrate and there are two types: simple and complex. Simple, or unhealthy, carbohydrates are produced when a natural plant food such as grain or wild rice is stripped of its germ and cellulose walls and transformed into white flour or white rice. The only reason for this stripping and transformation is to increase shelf life.

Because they do not have cell walls, when I eat them they are rapidly metabolized into glucose and are absorbed by my digestive system. This rapidity sends a high concentration of sugar into my blood stream causing my blood sugar to rise to unhealthy levels. My pancreas then responds by releasing insulin. High blood sugar also causes the proteins of my body to function less, which can age my immune system, arteries, and joints.

A widely used simple carbohydrate is sugar, which was, and to a certain extent still is, my poison of choice. I wasn't surprised to learn that sugar is addictive because I have always felt that I was hooked on my chocolate bars and desserts. I think of myself as being a sugarholic or a chocoholic.

Not only is sugar in all high-calorie baked goods, it is in most of the prepared and packaged foods I buy. I have found sugar disguised and listed in many forms and under many names: brown sugar, fructose, glucose, dextrose, corn syrup, raw sugar, high-fructose corn syrup, invert sugar, caramel, corn sweetener, dextrin, confectioner's sugar, and barley malt. Just about every food on the store shelves has a certain amount of sugar in it.

Five of the most common foods I've gotten my sugar from are: sweetened baked goods such as sugary cereals, muffins, and cakes; chocolate bars; ice cream; sweetened fruit drinks which could give me 20 to 30gms (0.7-1.0 oz) of sugar in one cup; and the highest ranking sugar intake was from my cola. In a 567 ml (20 oz) serving of soda pop there may be up to 85gms of sugar, which relates to about 3 ounces.

I should consume no more than 50gms (1.8 oz) of sugar a day and there are 4gms (0.14 oz) of sugar in one teaspoon. However, I was devouring as much as 200gms (7 oz or 50 teaspoons) a day from my soda, and from the processed, canned, and packaged foods that I also ate. When I looked at the equivalent calories of about 800, it scared me. And not only was I getting absolutely zero benefits in return, I was damaging every part of my body right down to my mitochondria, which are the powerhouses of my cells.

As explained by the Canadian Cancer Society sugar may cause certain cancers and when a person has cancer, the tumour feeds and thrives on sugar. I now think that my years of overeating everything sweet may have been a contributing factor to my breast cancer.

I discovered that when I eat sugar in my food it raises the amount of sugar in my blood for at least one to two hours. When consumed, sugar is broken down into simple sugar components and these are converted to glucose which is absorbed more quickly in my intestine. Even natural sugar like molasses, honey, and maple syrup raise blood sugar and supply empty calories.

Eating sugar increases the rate at which my body excretes calcium. Too much sugar in my blood destroys the natural protective control my body has over the usual everyday fluctuations in blood pressure. Also, high blood sugar causes an increase in triglyceride levels in my blood. The constant need for the pancreas to secrete insulin eventually exhausts it and I could ultimately develop diabetes. Since 1935, diabetes in North America has skyrocketed an astonishing 750%, almost on par with our increase in sugar consumption.

My body needs constant blood levels of glucose to function properly. However, it is better for me to stick to natural foods that have their own sugars. Fruit and some vegetables like sweet potatoes and beets contain unaltered fructose, and milk has lactose. These can give my body the sugars it needs for glucose. These foods also offer nutrients rather than empty calories.

Most nutrition experts believe that moderate sugar consumption is okay. But the definition of moderate to one person is different from the definition of moderate to another. If we eat too many sweets, our blood sugars rise too high, our body compensates by increasing the amount of insulin, our blood sugars then drop quickly causing fatigue and even more hunger. So really even a small amount is not good.

My body has no use for refined, or simple, carbohydrates. It's too bad that they are in just about every type of processed, packaged, canned, and manufactured food I buy. Since white flour is the main ingredient in most baked goods and pastries, when I eat them I am getting almost no fibre. Also, these disrupt my body's metabolism and hormones levels by providing pure energy with no nutrients. In order to compensate, my body will drain nutrients from my vigorous cells.

A downward health spiral that is definitely not conducive to living a long life.

I did my own personal study one day when I took a residential care aide course in my early fifties. We were having a small party with a cake. I tested my blood sugar level after eating my lunch and it was 4.8. I ate a piece of cake then tried again about half an hour later. My glucose level had risen to 5.6.

Since learning how bad simple carbohydrates are for me I have been trying to eat more complex or genuine carbohydrates which are found in foods that are in the same whole condition they were when grown. In this natural state the cells are still living inside the membrane of cellulose. Many complex carbohydrates such as grains, seeds, nuts, and beans will grow if planted. These carbohydrates are high in fibre, nutrients, and vitamins and are found in products such as whole grain breads and pastas, certain cereals, vegetables, legumes, beans, and some fruits.

They have the same calorie count as simple carbohydrates, but they are slower in breaking down in my body; they use more metabolic energy during digestion; they help stabilize my blood sugar levels; and when my body needs energy it goes to the carbohydrates first.

Sadly, in spite of learning about the evils of sugar I did not immediately stop drinking my colas. I was truly addicted to the sugar, and probably the caffeine. Over my cola drinking years, though, I did try to curb my sugar intake by buying diet cola.

Saccharin is the oldest artificial sugar substitute. It was discovered in 1878 but didn't come into heavy use until the sugar shortages during World War II. It has 300 times the sweetness of sucrose, but I found it left a bitter aftertaste in my mouth. In 1977, it was banned in Canada when studies showed there was a relationship between saccharin and some cancers. That year, in the United States, the company producing it was required to put warnings that it was a potential carcinogen on its packages. Those warning requirements have since been revoked and Health Canada is considering allowing it to be used as a sweetener in certain foods.

Then there were the drinks with sucralose, a synthetic compound discovered in 1976 by British scientists trying to make a new pesticide formula. While some scientists believe the molecule in sucralose is close to the molecule of sugar, others assert that it more closely resembles a pesticide. Although tests have shown that the substitute has caused shrunken thymus glands and enlarged liver and kidneys in rodents, there is nothing conclusive about its effects on humans. Some side effects of using sucralose, which I never experienced, may be muscle aches, headaches, dizziness, skin irritations, intestinal cramping, and stomach pains.

Aspartame was discovered in 1965 by a chemist looking for an anti-ulcer drug. It was approved to be introduced into foods in Canada in 1981. In the United States it was added to dry goods in 1981 and to carbonated drinks in 1983. When I first heard about aspartame it was touted as being harmless to humans because it was so close to being like natural sugar. I thought that finally I would be able to drink my cola without taking in too many calories. Instead, I developed a headache every time I had a glass.

I later heard that research showed aspartame could cause headaches. But then someone associated with the company manufacturing the sugar substitute stated that most of the people who drank diet pop were also on diets and that was probably the cause of their headaches. Well, in my case that wasn't true.

I finally quit buying diet cola all together because I figured that sugar, as bad as it was for me, was better than any of the substitutes.

When I really looked at my cola consumption I couldn't believe that I was drinking at least 72gms of sugar each day. Just the thought of putting eighteen actual teaspoons of sugar, one after the other, into my mouth makes my stomach turn, and yet I drank at least two cans of cola a day for thirty-five years. There are almost sixteen calories in 4gms (1 tsp) of sugar and when I add that to the other foods I ate like chocolate bars, cakes, etc. each day, I am horrified.

I thought about the trauma to my body when I ate high-sugar food, high-fat foods. I began to look at the cookies, cakes, pies, and chips, and to realize how damaging they were for me. I began to study the way I felt after I ate the wrong foods. My stomach was bloated. Sometimes, my balance seemed off, not so much like I was going to fall, but like I was disoriented. My spirits dropped. My whole body felt sick. But what I noticed the most was that I had no energy. I would wake up tired and think it was because I didn't sleep well. Now I know better, and I am really concerned about what such inferior food was doing to my heart and other organs.

After all my reading I now realize how much it was costing me, both in physical and monetary terms, to make myself sick and wreck my health. When I recall that I used to think having a piece of cake or pie or a bunch of cookies was treating myself, was rewarding myself, I wonder at what type of fool I was. I know now that each bite could have been shortening my life and that I was slowly killing myself.

I believe that taking responsibility, like common sense, is becoming a lost art. If I go into a bakery and buy ten doughnuts and eat them, it is not the bakery's fault that I get sick. What I willingly do, I am responsible for.

So, it is not the food I condemn; it is the way I ate the food that I blame. It is amazing how easily and quickly I traded the well-being of my body for the taste of chocolate cake, apple pie, doughnuts, or chocolate bars. How willing I was to feel sick in the future for the pleasure of the moment. When my body dies, I die, yet I have failed miserably to feed it properly.

It can take from ten to twenty years for the excessive intake of sugar to affect health and bring about a chronic illness. Over that length of time, eating too much sugar could cause weight gain, degeneration of muscles, dysfunction of the immune system, cardiovascular problems, arteriosclerosis, high blood pressure, heart disease, and premature aging.

Excessive sugar intake can also cause insulin resistance (where my tissues stop responding as they are supposed to when the pancreas produces insulin), diabetes, and hypoglycemia.

I feel so lucky that, over the years, my glucose fasting has remained around 4.4, well within the normal range of 3.3-6.0.

I also learned about my pH (proportion of hydrogen). It is important to my health that my body fluids remain within an acid/alkaline range. A pH of less than 7 is considered acidic while over 7 is alkaline. Different parts of my body have different pH balances. My stomach fluid has a pH of 1.5 while my pancreatic fluid is 8.8. Although one book suggested my blood pH should be between 7.35 and 7.45, according to my blood test results the range is between 5.0 and 8.5 and I am at 8, on the alkaline side.

One of the scariest reports I read was about cola soft drinks which contain phosphoric acid. Regular and diet colas have a very low acidic pH of around 2.5. To show what this means, if I take the normal pH of a substance to be 7 then a decrease of 1 in pH means that the acid level is increased tenfold. Another decrease of 1 pH means that the acid level increases by another tenfold or 100 times the normal rate. So, a substance with a pH of 5 is one hundred times more acidic than one that is at 7.

In order to neutralize the phosphoric acid in the cola, I would have to drink 3200 glasses of alkaline water with a pH of 8, 320 glasses with a pH of 9, or 32 glasses of water with a pH of 10.

My body has two ways to prevent acidic poisoning when I drink cola. One is to use alkaline blood shock absorbers to neutralize the acid. The other is to convert the acid into a less-reactive solid state by using calcium to change it to phosphates. The downside of those is that they could form calcified kidney stones or calcium deposits. If my body did nothing to counteract the acid in the cola, I would die immediately of acidic poisoning from drinking the first glass.

Studies by the United States National Library of Medicine shows that too much phosphorus can diminish the amount of calcium in my body and cause bone loss potentially leading to osteoporosis and heart disease.

All this information alarmed me, and I quit drinking cola. I'd like to say that I never started again. But that wouldn't be true. I watched a program about a 103 year old woman who was asked what she thought was the reason for her longevity. She held up a can of cola and said she'd been drinking one of them every day for years. I grasped onto that like a drowning person would a lifesaver. I knew that drinking cola was bad for me, but I still went back to drinking it after hearing her story. After all, if it didn't harm her, it shouldn't harm me.

There were times when I stopped again but I kept going back. Finally, I limited myself to one can a day and substituted a pot of green tea for the rest. But I still have moments when I try to quit.

***

Another simple carbohydrate is alcohol. Even though I went to parties every weekend when I was a teenager I was almost thirty before I began having the occasional drink and there are two reasons for that. First, I didn't really care for the taste of any alcoholic drink I was given and second because I knew that I have an addictive nature when it comes to something I like. I was afraid that if I did find something I enjoyed I would, as I do with food, over-indulge. Then I discovered the liqueurs Irish Cream and Kahlua.

They offered me the sweet taste that I liked.

Alcohol is toxic to my brain. When I drink a lot of it, it can impair the absorption of nutrients from my food, create inflammation in my systems and cause dehydration. My electrolyte balance, as well as my brain chemistry balance, is thrown off by dehydration which may result in dementia, dizziness, and blackouts, or even kidney failure. Molecules in alcohol can damage cell plasma membrane and parts of the interior of my cells. It also can cause the small blood vessels just under my skin to widen so more blood flows through them. This can lead to broken capillaries on my skin and could give my face a pinkish/red colour.

Excessive use of alcohol affects my brain creating slurred speech, loss of balance, slower reaction time, and some memory loss. Over consumption for a long period of time may lead to permanent mental conditions that require institutionalized care. Too much alcohol can be deadly to my body. It changes the metabolism of my liver which can cause many problems, such as cirrhosis of the liver, if taken over a long period of time.

Alcohol is harder on women than men. Once alcohol is digested it is dissolved into the water of my body. Men weigh more than women, so they have more water available for the dispersal of the alcohol they consume. This means a woman's brain and other organs are exposed to more alcohol than a man's.

As I age my body's ability to process alcohol is reduced mainly because an older person's body has less water.

In the past, there was evidence that alcohol in moderation, that is two or less drinks a day, could have some benefits. However, the Canadian government now recommends that people should have no more than two drinks a week. This would be a 341ml (12oz) bottle of 5% beer, a 43ml (5oz) shot glass of 40% hard liquor, or a 142ml (5oz) glass of twelve percent wine.

Red wine is especially good because it is full of flavonoids, which act as antioxidants and aid in our body's biological process. All grapes have resveratrol in their skins. When red wine is made, the juice has contact with the grape skins and that gives the wine its colour. Therefore, the wine has resveratrol in it, which is believed to slow down immune system aging and provides anti-cancer benefits.

Unfortunately, I am not a big fan of wine.

Because I always add milk, and/or cream, to those liqueurs I like, I say that I am getting my calcium and Vitamin D. And, because the milk and/or cream is filling, I cannot drink enough to make me drunk.

After what I learned about how alcohol affects my body, though, I am glad that my drinking usually consisted of one or two drinks when we had company and maybe an average of one a month the rest of the time, except at Christmas.

* * *

Fats, fats, fats. Are they good for me? Are they bad for me? It depends on the author of the book or the scientist who conducted and interpreted the study.

There are two types of fats: dietary and body. A certain amount of dietary fat intake is essential to my body's wellbeing. Too little or too much, though, will impair its ability to look after itself. My body digests and processes dietary fat from foods into energy, or into hormones, or for cell walls, or whatever it needs. Or, unhappily, it can store it as body fat. This body fat results from more calories being taken in than are burned off.

Fat and plaque build-up is the leading cause of arterial aging and eventually cardiovascular disease. As many as 50% of North Americans could be affected by cardiovascular disease and 40% of those will die. It is the major cause of heart attacks, strokes, some types of kidney disease, memory loss, impotence, and wrinkles. Even if the disease is mild, it will make people feel tired and old.

There is a saying in the medical field that "we are as old as our arteries." Therefore, it is sad that as early as July 2000 ABC News reported that, with North America's overall poor diet and lack of exercise, plaque had already been found in the arteries of teenagers.

There are five different dietary fats: saturated, monounsaturated, polyunsaturated, trans-fats, and triglycerides.

Fats are made up of hydrogen, carbon, and a little oxygen, all of which are termed fatty acids. If a fat contains all the hydrogen it can hold it is said to be saturated with hydrogen. Any fat that is hard at room temperature but liquefies when heated, like butter, lard, or some margarines, is a saturated fat.

Having too much hydrogen is detrimental to my body. Saturated fats lower the good HDL (high-density lipoprotein) in my blood and raise the lousy LDL (low-density lipoprotein.) Fried foods and deep fried foods are hard on my liver, heart, kidneys, and brain. Contrary to what I had always thought, saturated fats, not dietary cholesterol, is the largest contributor to an elevated level of cholesterol in my body.

What is bad for my body is also bad for my mind. Not only can saturated fats clog the arteries to my heart they can also clog the arteries to my brain and may cause a stroke. I certainly don't want to live a long life without being mentally alert.

Unsaturated fats are found in plants and are liquid at room temperature. The "mono" and "poly" prefixes indicate the chemical structure of the oils. Monounsaturated fats and oils are in olives, olive oils, cold pressed canola oil, flaxseed, and nuts. Polyunsaturated fats and oils come from corn, soybeans, and most vegetables. Both actually help reduce heart disease and cancers, if taken in the proper amounts.

There are nine calories per gram, or 120 calories per tablespoon, in fat. That is more than twice the amount of calories in a gram of protein or carbohydrate.

When I was a child I remember Mom buying solid white margarine in a plastic bag with a small packet of colouring attached on the inside. She would hand one of the packages to me to mix. I would break the packet and begin squeezing the bag with my hands to spread the yellow colour around. At first it was tough going because the margarine was hard but eventually the repeated squeezing by my warm hands softened it enough to mix.

I was a teenager when I first heard that margarine had half the calories of butter. Bonus! Margarine became my fat of choice. As I was raising my family I bought the solid margarine, at first because that was all that was available and then because it was cheaper than soft margarine or butter. I now know that the calorie count is the same in both margarine and butter, but it was a good advertising ploy that sold a lot of harmful product.

Trans-fats or trans-fatty acids, also called the hidden fats, are formed when unsaturated fats, like vegetable oils are pumped with hydrogen. This creates fats that, like saturated fats, are solid at room temperature but liquid when heated. These fats alter my body's metabolic process, and many scientists think that the artificial molecular structure of trans-fats can cause more damage than the natural molecules of saturated fats. Trans-fats can harm my arteries by increasing my LDL or bad cholesterol levels. The more I eat of them, the faster my body will show signs of disease and age.

When I looked at the nutritional facts on the back of the pouch of those chocolate covered peanut butter balls that I binged on for so long, I saw that eighteen pieces totalled 220 calories and provided 41% of my daily intake of saturated and trans-fats. There were 109 pieces in a package, and I ate them all. That works out to 1320 calories and 246% of my daily intake of saturated and trans-fats.

I read that just a 2% increase in my calorie intake from trans-fats could cause my coronary risk to jump 93%. When I look at that it's a wonder that I am still alive.

Now I know that when the hydrogenated or partially hydrogenated oils are listed before the polyunsaturated and monounsaturated fats, the product is high in trans-fats. Many companies are trying to cut down on trans-fats in their products but there is still a lot of it in our foods.

Trans-fats give food a longer shelf life and are in most packaged goods. Even if foods are advertised as being saturated fat or cholesterol free, they could still have trans-fats in them.

So now I wonder when I will know if I have done any damage to my body because of my diet high in trans-fats. Will it be when I am eighty and have a stroke and have to live the rest of my life in a home?

In order to prevent any further damage, I now avoid the bad fats as much as possible. I do not buy margarine anymore but do have butter in my house. I would rather get my calories from natural butter than from unnatural margarine. I do use it sparingly, though, because it is a saturated fat.

Triglycerides are another type of fat in my body. Sugar, trans-fats, saturated fats, refined grains, starchy foods, alcohol, and high calorie foods can raise triglyceride levels in my body, and they are used to store fat. High triglyceride levels can age my arteries.

Since most of my eating has included all of the above fats, over the years when I had my blood tests done I asked about my triglyceride levels. I was astonished to learn that they are 0.55, well within the range of 0.45-2.29.

Cholesterol is a feared word by most people, me included. For years we were warned to stay away from any food that contained cholesterol. However, about 90% of the cholesterol in my body is manufactured by my liver. A friend of mine was told she had high cholesterol, and she should cut back on eggs. This she did for two months and when she went back to be tested her cholesterol was still high. She went home and scrambled up three eggs for her lunch.

Cholesterol is used by my body to produce hormones and build cell walls. It is a special type of fat found in my cells, my brain, and in my blood, and it acts as a fat transportation system. It is also an important compound in the production of bile. This bile helps break down and digest the fats from my meals so I am able to absorb them.

Cholesterol is also found in the foods I eat and much of it is not needed. The larger the amount of fat and outside cholesterol in my system, the more cholesterol my liver has to make and the more bile I need.

There are two, one-way messengers that circulate cholesterol in my body: HDL, also known as good cholesterol, and LDL, a.k.a. lousy cholesterol. The LDLs move cholesterol from my liver to my organs and tissues and could leave some of it sticking to the walls of my blood vessels as plaque. Over time this becomes known as hardening of the arteries.

The HDLs are more efficient. They whisk the cholesterol back to my liver without any left over. The higher the number of HDLs taking the cholesterol to my liver and the less LDLs transporting it out to the blood vessels the better it is for me.

Since HDLs and LDLs are so important I asked my doctor what mine were. He gave me a copy of them. My cholesterol is within normal range. My LDLs are lower than average. My HDLs are high.

I was astonished considering my eating habits. One bit of good news I also learned is, if my LDLs are low enough, my body will pull any deposits of fats and cholesterol from my artery walls. I can actually reverse any damage done to my heart, and my vessels will be smoother, more elastic, and open. I can halt any aging of my arteries and heart.

This gives me another component to add to the plus side on my quest to live to 120 years-of-age.

Chapter 5
Free Radicals and Antioxidants

Oxygen is necessary for my body to function. But it is also a deadly poison. Oxygen does its damage by oxidizing with the *dietary fat* I consume to form unpaired molecules called free radicals. It is on the same principle as metal rusting or food going rancid. It is disconcerting to know that for every hundred molecules of oxygen that I breathe, two or three become free radicals.

My body wants my negative and positive charged molecules to be equal in my cells. So, these oxygen-caused unpaired free radical molecules can do a lot of indiscriminate damage to my systems by trying to give a free electron to another molecule or by taking one. While this stabilizes the first free radical, it makes the other molecule unstable and it in turn goes looking to hook up with another cell. Free radicals can attack just about every type of cell in my body. They can distort some of the information in my cells; they can overcrowd my cell membranes; they can support the growth of cancer cells; and they can impair the work of my mitochondria, which are the energy factories of my cells.

Each day, every one of my cells could have as many as 10,000 free radical hits, which depletes the cells of their energy and therefore less new cells are reproduced. The resulting slower cell multiplication could age my body. Most of the harm is repaired by my body but over time free radical injury may accumulate in my cells and tissues, and this in turn could contribute to my aging process.

Meat, eggs, dairy foods, processed meat, saturated fats, polyunsaturated oils, hydrogenated vegetable oils, and most commercial baked goods will age my body by putting a strain on my organs and on my digestive and cardiovascular systems. They also introduce free radicals into my body. I am sorry to say that most of my meals during my first sixty-some years contained an abundance of the above ingredients, and my body must have had to work overtime to get rid of the free radicals. I wonder what harm those years did to my organs and systems that won't appear until later in my life.

Free radicals might also be to blame for the damage that cholesterol does to my body. Researchers have shown in laboratories that body cells balk at picking up cholesterol in its normal form, but once free radicals cause the cholesterol to oxidize, cells quickly absorb it.

Fried hamburger has a greater amount of free radicals than most foods. Broiling or charbroiling meats contributes to the formation of more free radicals than if they are baked, boiled, or steamed. Cooking any flesh food, including fish, to the well-done stage produces carcinogens called heterocyclic amines.

When foods are fried in polyunsaturated vegetable oils, they become loaded with free radicals. This is particularly true if the oil is reheated over and over again. Once the oil is changed, though, the cycle begins again. Free radical heaven. Frying any type of food, even vegetables, also promotes the formation of free radicals. Baking, boiling, or steaming them is best.

Years ago, I heard the statement that we all have cancer cells in our body and, of course, I didn't believe it because I figured if it were true we would all be dead. But now I know that every day cancer cells are initiated, that is take the first step towards becoming cancerous, in my body by means of the food I eat or from toxins I breathe and it is only through the grace of my body's ability to kill these cells that I am still living.

The more foods I consume that encourage free radicals, the more activated cancer cells my body produces and the greater the burden on my immune system. The daily task of destroying a huge number of unnecessary cancer cells frequently overloads and weakens it.

As much as one-third of all cancers can be attributed to diet and most of that is from foods that cause free radicals. If I eat a high saturated fat diet, my liver produces more bile and as this bile breaks down, free radicals are released that may eventually cause colon cancer.

Antioxidants protect my cells from the free radicals and my body does have its own antioxidant defence system for controlling, or fighting and disarming them. Every cell produces an enzyme, or scavenger, to break down free radicals. However, their effectiveness can be helped and increased by the antioxidants I obtain from my food and by exercising.

Foods high in antioxidants are fish and fish oil, liver, heart, kidney, goat cheese, and milk, and green, red, purple, orange, and yellow fruits and vegetables like spinach, peppers, carrots, the cabbage family, turnip greens, sweet potato, tomato, berries, and melons. Green tea is also an antioxidant.

Without enough antioxidants, injured cells will accumulate and harm my arteries and immune system. This damage could lead to such problems as strokes, heart disease, cancer, cataracts, and memory loss. The more foods I eat that contain antioxidants and anti-carcinogens, the less chance I have that free radicals will overload my immune system and produce cancer in my body.

All foods from plants, except palm and coconut nut oils, are low in fat and rarely promote free radicals. Canola, flaxseed, and olive oils are mainly monounsaturated oils and produce few free radicals. Vegetables, fruits, and whole grains are all protectors against many diseases.

Dark chocolate is now thought to be a healthy food. It contains antioxidants called flavonoids, which are also found in vegetables and fruits. A potent member of these flavonoids in chocolate is epicatechin. Flavonoids work to lower my blood pressure and cholesterol, help reduce the risk of blood clots and clogged arteries, and boost my immune system.

Eating chocolate, or even just smelling it, activates the pleasure sensors of my brain. I like the taste, so consuming it relaxes me and gives me a feeling of euphoria.

The fat in chocolate is from steraic acid, which my body likens to the healthy monounsaturated fat. But that doesn't mean I can overindulge as I have most of my life. Too much fat from any source is not good for me. Plus, most chocolates have sugar in them.

High quality dark chocolate with nuts gives the most benefits. Milk chocolate and chocolate ice cream have too many calories and most of them are from animal fats and sugar. They also contain few flavonoids because they have been processed out of the chocolate. White chocolate usually contains cocoa butter, sugar, milk, and flavourings.

It was amazing to learn that white flour, white bread, sugar, and all sweeteners produce few free radicals. But they are also low in nutrients and have lots of empty calories. Plus, they are normally combined with high fat in products, so the free radicals are there. Non-fat dairy products also do not produce many free radicals and they are good for you.

Unfortunately, as I age my body's production of antioxidants may slow and it could absorb them less efficiently.

There is good news, though. Not all free radicals are bad. The white blood cells of my immune system use free radicals to help kill bacteria and viruses. They take advantage of the free radicals' desire to attach to anything to kill those invaders and they save me from many diseases.

Chapter 6
Fibre and Water

Like most people I have gone through bouts of constipation, which looking at my diet, is not a shock. I was seventeen when I first heard that constipation could eventually lead to colon cancer. I immediately went to my doctor about it, but instead of explaining what I needed to do to change it, he prescribed pills for me to take. It was years before I learned more.

Dietary fibre, also known as bulk or roughage, is found in the parts of vegetables, fruits, grains, legumes, and nuts that my body does not digest or absorb. Therefore, it passes virtually unchanged through my stomach, small intestine, and into my colon.

Fibre is either soluble or insoluble. Soluble fibre dissolves in water to form a material similar to jelly. In my body, it slows down the emptying of my stomach, which helps moderate the absorption of sugar, and it lowers glucose and cholesterol levels. Oats have the highest proportion of soluble fibre of all the grains. Other foods include beans, barley, rice bran, peas, citrus fruit, strawberries, and apples.

Insoluble fibre has no calories and does not dissolve in water. It is not broken down by the bacteria of my digestive system and passes through the intestines intact. It increases stool bulk and aids in the movement of meal remnants through my digestive system. Insoluble fibre doesn't lower cholesterol, but it helps regulate metabolism and digestion, stabilizes blood glucose levels, and slows the absorption of foods. It is found in grapefruit, grapes, raisins, sweet potatoes, and peas.

In my thirties I read about a high fibre diet and how it would keep me regular. I tried it for a while but oh, the flatulence. It did work wonders on my bowel movement: three meals in, three meals out. But it was very hard to sustain, and I soon quit. I didn't like that there were no chocolate bars, cookies, or ice cream on the menu.

I now understand that a high fibre diet helps rid my body of waste products faster. It also lowers the production of cancer causing bile acids. By eating a low fibre diet I was carrying the remains of up to eleven meals in my colon. This slower processing resulted in a bowel transit time of three days which meant the cancer causing agents remained in my bowels longer.

So, for my life up to and including some of my fifties I was playing Russian roulette with colon cancer. Then I found out that there is a history of pre-cancerous colon polyps in our family. However, it still took another three years before I finally went and had a colonoscopy. My bowels were fine, and I didn't need another one until I was sixty-five. That one, too, was clean as was the one when I was seventy.

I have never been much of a water drinker. To me it has no flavour. I have always preferred milk, juice, or a cola drink to quench my thirst.

Water is in every cell and tissue of my body and plays a vital role in the function of all my systems. Virtually every living process requires water for the chemical events essential to life. Water enables me to maintain my normal body temperature. Waste products are carried out of my body through water.

Water is the conduit of the electrical messages my brain sends to my body. Without enough water these messages are compromised. I need water to build the cells, tissues, and organs of my body. And since every organ can only function according to its level of hydration, insufficient water means my body only has the amount of energy that its state of hydration will allow.

All my nutrients are delivered with the use of water. A deficiency in water means a deficiency in nutrients. My digestive system requires water to help make enzymes and to carry them where they are needed. Plus, water is important for removing the toxins from my body through my skin, bladder, and bowels.

If my cells are properly hydrated my pH will be balanced, my fat burning capabilities will increase, I will have less free-radical damage, and my immunity will be strengthened. When I realized how important water is to my body and brain, I changed my drinking habits. I have a tall glass of water as soon as I get up in the morning.

My body is made up of two-thirds water. But how much water do I really need? And what type is best? Again, the results garnered from studies contradict each other.

Back in the 1940s government guidelines recommended 1 millilitre of water for each calorie of food eaten, which worked out to 1.89- 2.3 litres (64-80 oz) per day. However, the word "water" encompassed the total daily fluid intake from all sources. Some authors reported that my body doesn't care where that fluid comes from as long as it gets it. So, I obtain fluids from the foods I eat, and whatever I drink, including pop, can count towards my daily supply.

Others recommended the average adult consume about two quarts of water per day and that soft drinks, coffee, tea, juices, and alcohol cannot replace water.

I believe the following: my body has its own hydration control called thirst, which operates through hormones and senses in my vascular system. It lets me know I need more water by making me thirsty. Therefore, I should drink only when I feel thirsty.

We are also advised not to drink too much fluid because if we take in more than our kidneys can process, we may develop a condition called, "water intoxication" also known as hyponatremia or hyper-hydration. It occurs when the level of sodium, an electrolyte that regulates our body's fluids, is diluted by over-consumption of water in a short period of time. Usually, our kidneys get rid of any excess water, but if they can't, then the water causes cells in our body to swell and malfunction. Symptoms include headache, confusion, coma, and eventually death.

The type of water is also debated in the books. Pure water is the best to drink but it is almost impossible to find. Some say distilled water is the next best for us. However, others call that dead water because it has no minerals in it. Drinking two quarts of distilled water a day could leach some of the normal minerals from my body.

Natural spring water may be filtered or treated. Tap water is said to be the worst water to drink. It has chlorine, fluoride, biological poisons, and pollutants in it. There is increasing evidence that fluoride, while good for teeth, is particularly harmful to bones. When used over a lifetime it may aggravate osteoporosis and cause bones to become brittle. Chlorine in our water interferes with the absorption of iodine and it may convert the contaminants into carcinogens. On the other hand, chlorine is needed to kill the bacteria in our water.

It doesn't look like we can win.

Chapter 7
Vitamins and Supplements

Occasionally over my adult life I have tried vitamins and minerals. These periods did not last long mainly because I would forget to take them. There is still some doubt that vitamins do any good. A few of the authors of the books advised me to take a multivitamin, some gave a list of vitamins and minerals that are a must to take, others give long lists of supplements that the authors feel are necessary for me. Some authors said they are not required, and then there are those who advised me to get all my nutrients from the food I eat.

There is also a dispute over what type of vitamins I should be taking and how much. A few books stated that if I take them I only need a small amount. Others want me to take mega-doses of specific types. Certain vitamins and minerals, though, may be toxic to my body if taken in excess.

Vitamins A and D, if consumed in too high a dosage can cause medical problems. One study showed that taking Vitamin E, A, and beta carotene did not increase longevity.

In fact, too much may cause early death. Other vitamins, if not needed, are just excreted in my urine.

It has been shown that most elder adults have insufficient levels of Vitamin D. This could be because they wear more clothing, they use sun block, and they stay indoors more. Also, their skin may not be able to synthesize the vitamin.

Since Vitamin D is fat soluble, in heavier people much of the vitamin manufactured from the sun by their skin is trapped in their excess fat cells and their body can't utilize it.

There are food-based and synthetic vitamins on the market. It is believed by some researchers that our body looks upon synthetic supplements as a toxin and it uses a lot of energy and enzymes to break them down.

For every study that shows they are necessary, there is another one that concludes people taking vitamins are no healthier than those who do not take them. No one could find any evidence, though, that taking vitamins would increase my longevity.

One important fact to remember is that besides the vitamins and minerals I get from the food I eat, there are also micronutrients in the fruits and vegetables I consume that are important to my body. They help prevent blood clots and heart attacks, lessen the development of blood vessels in tumours, and slow my body's aging process. These I will not find in supplements.

Also, vitamins will not offset an unhealthy lifestyle.

My body does manufacture some vitamins but not vitamin C, which is critical in the synthesis of collagen, a substance that helps cement my cells together. We humans lack the enzyme, gulonolactone oxidase, which is needed to make it. We also cannot manufacture minerals, so we have to get them from our diet.

It is believed that our ancestors lost their ability to produce Vitamin C when they started eating fruits and vegetables high in that vitamin and their body didn't need to manufacture it anymore. If that is true, then I am wondering if our bodies will eventually stop absorbing the vitamins and minerals from our food if we take supplements in pill form, if we make the work easy for our system. Is it a question of use it or lose it?

Salt is a mineral that helps regulate my body's fluid balance and one of my basic tastes is for salt. When I crave something salty, that may be because I have a mineral deficiency or an insufficient supply of salt itself.

Salt has been used for consumption, preservation of foods, seasoning, and even as a medium of exchange in place of money since ancient times. It is usually harvested from sea water or rock deposits. It is a mineral composed of 40% sodium and 60% chloride and is necessary for all animal life.

My mother cooked our vegetables with salt, but because we did not buy canned or packaged foods when I was growing up, there were little hidden salts in my diet. As an adult I don't use salt to cook with and seldom put any extra on my food. However, I do buy more foods that have salt in them, since it seems almost impossible not to do so.

Fresh, natural food has little salt. All the salt we eat is what we add to our foods and what is added by companies to all processed foods. It comes in various forms; refined or table salt, unrefined or sea salt, and iodized salt which has had iodine added to it. It also comes under the name of sodium chloride and sodium benzoate.

Table salt is the most commonly used salt today. It is prepared from rock salt, the deposits of which were formed by the drying up of ancient seas. The salt is then refined to purify it and improve its storage and handling characteristics. This involves making a brine solution and treating it with chemicals that get rid of most of the magnesium and calcium salts, both of which give it a bitter taste. After that it goes through many evaporation stages to collect pure sodium chloride crystals, and these are kiln dried.

Since the 1950s, an anti-caking agent sodium hexcyanoferrate II has been added to the brine. This makes the crystals irregular. More anti-caking agents such as aluminosilicate and alumino-calcium silicate are added after crystallization to absorb humidity. Concerns have been raised about these two agents since they contain aluminum. Too much salt could lead to an excess of aluminum in our system.

Potassium iodide, used to prevent iodine deficiency diseases such as thyroid gland problems and endemic goiter, is also added to make iodized salt and then it is packaged for sale.

Sea salt is obtained from the evaporation of water usually in small basins using the sun. Some people believe that unrefined salt is healthier than table salt. However, it may not contain enough iodine.

There are many health problems associated with too much salt in diets. These range from heartburn, to osteoporosis, high blood pressure, to gastric cancer. An excess of salt causes blood vessels to tighten. This increases blood pressure, which is a leading risk factor for cardiovascular diseases. It is estimated that each year in Canada, there are at least 17,000 cases of stroke, heart attack, and heart failure due to too much salt intake. That is like all the citizens of a small city suddenly becoming disabled or dying.

Sodium, along with calcium, magnesium, and potassium, is one of the electrolytes necessary in our body but we should have no more than 1500 mgs (0.05

oz) of salt a day. Too bad most of us are eating about 3500 mgs (0.12 oz).

If people cut their sodium consumption in half there would be up to 20% fewer major strokes, 25% fewer cases of heart failure, and 7% less heart attacks a year.

Part Two
Aging and Factors That Affect It

Chapter 8
Aging and Theories On Aging

During my research I found a book about healthy aging. The author stated that gerontologists study old age and an increasing number of them believe that the human body is capable of living for 120 or even 150 years. They learned that animals tended to live six times the period needed to complete their growth. If we apply that to our species and we presume twenty years to be the age that our skeleton is finished growing, then we should be living to 120 years-of-age. If that is true, the author continued, then most of the human race, with our average life span of only around eighty years, was dying way too young.

I was intrigued, so I searched for other articles and books on the subjects of aging, longevity, the human body and how it works, and the effects aging will have on my body. Some books stressed that I had to go on hormone replacement therapy. A couple authors talked about nanotechnology, which is the study of objects whose smallest features are less than 100 nanometres (billionths of a metre). Researchers are building machines that size called nanobots. The authors predicted that in the future these nanobots will be used to go into our bodies and repair damage to our organs, which may eventually eliminate death totally.

The more I learned the more I wanted to learn so I also read newspapers and magazines, watched news programs and documentaries, and went on the Internet. I sought out information wherever I could find it.

In spite of all the data on the subject of aging, however, no one was able to make a definite statement on how I could live to a ripe elder age. Everyone used words like: studies show; seem to; papers suggest; and maybe. Although no author could give me a specific way of life that would guarantee I could actually live to 120, I did discover what I was doing, and had been doing for most of my life, that could potentially accelerate my aging process and shorten my life. I also found out that some of the things I had been doing were good for me.

One fact I did find out is that aging is not a disease nor something I should fear; it is a part of my growth, my life. It is something I have done since birth. It is to be expected. Aging itself, is painless. It is the diseases I could develop as I age that will cause the pain. And all those diseases can be prevented.

The authors were all quite adamant that I could do it, that I could actually live to 120 years-of-age. They cited that maximum life span is set by the age that the oldest person has been recorded as reaching. Madame Jeanne Calment was born on February 21, 1875 in Arles, France. She died on August 4, 1997 at age 122 years and 164 days. She claimed it was port wine, olive oil, exercise, and a sense of humour that made the difference. She had a brother and sister who died before she was born. Her other brother lived to ninety-seven years. Jeanne's only child, a daughter died at age thirty-six, and Jeanne's grandson also only lived to thirty-six.

Until someone can prove, through authentic birth or baptism certificates, that they have lived longer, for now 122 years and 164 days is how long we, the human species, should expect to live.

Longevity is the length or duration of life. My longevity will be how close I get to the maximum life of 122 years and 164 days before I die. Sixty-five, the age I had set for my death, was just over halfway there.

Someone dying in their eighties, which is considered a normal duration of life, has only reached three-quarters of their life span.

By this time, I had smiled at my teenage naivety and decided that age sixty-five was not an arbitrary termination number. Despite my year of cancer, mentally and physically I felt strong and healthy and if I could maintain that as I aged further then there was no need to end my life early. But could I actually live to 118 years-of-age and go to Canada's Bicentennial celebrations or to 120 years-of-age so I could tell everyone about my experience?

Some of the books gave the names of people who had reached 100 and beyond. I went onto the Internet to look them up and I found long lists of centenarians from many different countries. These people had done it unconsciously, without design. They hadn't worked at it.

What nagged at me, though, was that old person I didn't want to become, the one who was lonely, decrepit, lost, the one who had to be "adopted". As explained by some of the books, that old person could be avoided by the proper lifestyle.

One in ten thousand people is expected to reach at least one hundred years of age. Could I consciously do it? Could I reach that age and beyond by making changes to my lifestyle? And a bonus to those changes would be that I might be able to prevent a reoccurrence of cancer.

* * *

The topic of aging was never part of any of my school subjects. If it was raised at social or family gatherings it was always as a joke or someone describing their aches and pains. No one ever started a discussion on what aging meant to them. So, most of what I read about the aging process was new to me. I didn't know it was its own specialty science and that there had been so many studies done on it.

Nor did I know that scientists had a definition for aging or *senescence*. It is described as the overall mental and physical deterioration of the body as it gets older, the decline that people experience as they grow older. It is the process of growing old and approaching normal death.

What I do know is that when I was younger, that explanation is what I believed would happen to my body as I turned forty and fifty and sixty. I looked at older age as a time when I would be unable to do anything and my body and mind would fall apart. I would become stooped, slow, and overweight. The corresponding aging of my mind would make me forget things and be confused. Hence, my decision to commit suicide at sixty-five.

Scientists have compiled a list of what they term as signs of aging, like eye cataracts, hearing loss, hardening of the arteries, osteoporosis, and rising blood pressure and cholesterol. Everyone who ages, they decree, will suffer from one or more of these. They also maintain that there will be a decrease in muscle flexibility, stamina and endurance, and an increase in fat.

Having watched my dad reach his eighties and my mom reach her nineties without any of these signs occurring I was heartened when I read that aging doesn't have to be associated with bone fractures, dementia, or heart problems. Those features do affect some, but not all people as they grow older, and they are the result of diseases or from the disuse of their bodies. They are not results of aging and yet they are a label attached to elder age.

No one knows for sure how or why aging occurs. There is no one and only reason for aging, nor is there a one and only way of combating it. We will all age and how we do it will be different. Some of us will live a long and active life. Some of us won't.

We humans are the only species that understand what aging is and the only species that realize what is happening to our bodies. We are also the only ones who have developed a time frame in which we live our lives.

There are over three hundred different theories on aging, but I could not find one definite conclusion as to how and why we age.

Some scientists say that I have a genetic clock, which governs how long my cells will live under ideal circumstances, that is, if nothing damages them in any way. They think this clock is set to run for 120 years. Other researchers assert that my body has been programmed to self-destruct at a certain age.

The wear of existence theory states that outside forces, such as trauma, viruses and bacteria, free radicals, and toxins, started attacking my cells as soon as I was conceived and continue throughout my life. My cells grow increasingly overloaded with waste and chemical clutter and I start to look, act, and feel old.

Still another hypothesis proclaims that my body and cells are damaged by abuse and overuse. Then there is the one that proposes my aging depends on the genetic programming of my DNA. And the Membrane Hypothesis of Aging theory suggests that injury done to each cell's membrane over the years affects its function.

There are also many conjectures as to why I and everyone else on this planet age. There is the rate-of-living, also known as the live fast, die young theory. Everyone has a pre-set amount of time on this planet and when my time is up, I will die.

Another concept is about evolutionary aging. It is based on the idea that once I have passed on my genes to the next generation, I am no longer deemed necessary. Death comes through an accumulation of genetic defects as soon as the next generation has reached maturity. And this may be so when you look at the fact that my chances of developing a life threatening disease increases as I age. However, does this really have to happen? Some researchers believe it doesn't.

Then there are those who think that, through evolution, the human race generated the aging process to help mankind survive and prosper in an adverse environment. Over thousands of years, we introduced genetic changes so that each individual would have a limited life span. Since most of our major physiological systems peak when we are in our late twenties, those researchers assert that we were given just enough time to raise our children and prepare them for their reproductive years before dying.

Others disagree. They point out that since prehistoric times older people have been revered because of their knowledge of what had happened in the past. They knew where food was, what food was poisonous, what weather changes meant, where the best hunting grounds were, everything that the tribe or clan needed to know to survive. So aging was not developed by us but is something that happens to us.

Many scientists use mortality doubling as a better way to define aging. Mortality doubling is the amount of time needed to double the likelihood of death after a person reaches adulthood. In most industrialized countries that number is between seven and ten years after we reach the age of forty.

To explain how it works, let's take ten years as the mortality doubling number. When I reached fifty years-of-age I had twice the chances of dying than I had at forty. And when I turned sixty, I had four times the chance of dying than I had at forty. At seventy it was eight times and so on. This shows that as I get older my chances of dying become greater which, really, is not a surprise.

There are two ways in which I have been aging: physically and mentally. Unless I have a serious illness or become handicapped in some way, I should be able to control how fast I will age in the future.

My chronological age is what my actual calendar years are. From the minute I was born I have a chronological age that cannot be changed, even by lying.

My biological age is how old my body is. It is how well my body performs in comparison to others of my chronological age group. It is based on two features, my genes and my lifestyle. Genes, I am stuck with, but my biological age can be changed, for better or worse, by my lifestyle.

Some people's biological age is younger than their chronological age and for some unfortunate people it is older. Biological aging differs from chronological aging in that it is not uniform; that is, different areas of my body age at different rates. One part shrinks 6% between adulthood and older age while another area shrinks 45%. My digestive tract doesn't change much but my bladder and kidneys may. My sense of taste peaked at six years of age, my eyesight at ten, and bone density in my twenties.

So biological age is individual because everyone's body is unique.

Psychological age is how old I feel. This is personal and differs with each person. Since people don't age the same mentally and physically, it is up to each person to decide how he or she is aging. I did a mini triathlon at the age of fifty-seven, I have done 5K and 10K walk/runs, and I have backpacked a few times in my sixties. Now in my seventies I have been a dragon boat racer for over twenty years. Because of my ability to do these things I believe that so far I have aged well both physically and mentally. But so might my neighbour down the street who walks with a cane and is hard of hearing. It all comes down to perception.

Psychological aging is relative and can influence my biological age. At forty, I discovered that I didn't feel any older than I did at twenty. At fifty, I didn't feel any older than I did at forty. And sixty and seventy were no different.

Plus, even though sixty-five was my cut off point, I have always had a positive attitude about living. I love life. I enjoy living. But that could be because so far my body has been healthy. Would I enjoy life as much if my body had failed me in some way?

The concept of aging is hard to define but researchers have developed a list of signs that state a person is old. Two of them are loss of hearing and poor eyesight, both of which are caused by changes to that area of the body. However, not every elder person loses his or her hearing or eyesight. My mother had excellent hearing right up to her death at ninety-two, and I knew one woman who was still reading at ninety-eight and another at 103 years of age.

One point in my favour is that there have always been more women reaching elder age than men even though there are more male babies born than female.

The human egg has an X-chromosome. Half of the sperm that wriggle their way to the egg have the Y-chromosome, the other half have the X-chromosome. If the baby is a girl then the X sperm made it first to the egg; if a boy, the Y sperm arrived first. The Y-chromosomes are smaller than the X ones and travel more quickly. This means that more than half of the combinations result in boy foetuses.

However, male foetuses are more likely to undergo a spontaneous abortion so that only about 51% of babies born are male. Statistics show that when each generation reaches elder age, there are more women than men. And the reasons may be that in many societies there is a wide difference in the behaviour of men and women. Men tend to be more combative and therefore suffer more injuries. Some of them are more competitive in and out of work and that raises their stress levels. For many they work in physically dangerous jobs. In the past men smoked more than women and therefore were more prone to heart disease and cancer.

With the younger generations there is levelling out of male/female behaviour. Women now have the stress of working while running a household, more of them smoke, and they are going into typical male jobs, such as the armed forces and construction. There are also more men being stay-at-home fathers.

In the future there may be an equalization in male and female longevity, but for now I am glad to be a woman.

Chapter 9
Genetics

When I learned about genetics, I thought I had found the magic bullet that could guarantee elder age for me. It has been shown that people who live longer had parents who lived longer. No one knows for sure, however, how much this has to do with genes and how much it has to do with their education, having a positive outlook on life, their wealth, and their health.

My maternal grandmother lived to ninety-six, my mother to ninety-two. My father died at eighty-two, one of the youngest ages in his family. Most of my immediate ancestors have made it almost three-quarters of the way to their maximum life span.

Like everyone else in this world I have trillions of cells, which are called the building blocks of my body. Around the shell of each cell is a flexible membrane. At the core of the cell is the nucleus called the control centre. Inside the nucleus are my chromosomes. I inherited twenty-three chromosomes from my mother and the same number from my father, so I have a total of forty-six chromosomes. These pair up to make twenty-three sets.

Each set of my chromosomes has about 25,000 genes. Genes are the instructions or blueprints every organism needs to determine its characteristics. They are made up of a chemical called deoxyribonucleic acid or DNA. They use this DNA to form the words of the genetic instructions that oversee the behaviour of each and every cell in my body. DNA also controls the manufacture of materials called proteins. Just about everything in my body, such has muscles or hair, is made up of, or made by, these proteins.

Like my chromosomes, I received my genes from my parents, and they determined what I looked like (brown hair and blue eyes) and how I functioned. They gave directions for building every part of my body right from the time I was conceived. While I do have features from each of my parents, because there are millions of combinations of these genes I am totally unique. Some of my genes worked harder during childhood, while others are labouring for me every day of my life. My genes occur in exactly the same order in my chromosomes, and they also come in pairs.

So far over 4,000 hereditary diseases have been catalogued by scientists. However, they agree that we humans have no death gene. We are not programmed to die at a certain age. There is what is termed an anti-aging chromosome 4 that is more common in people who live to be 100 and over, but since only half of them have it, it really is not essential for longevity.

Every species on earth has its own set of genes. Just as a lion's genes predispose it to becoming a lion, so my genes predisposed me to becoming human.

The total genetic make-up of an organism, such as humans, is called our genome.

My grandfather on my mother's side, Sydney Relf, had high blood pressure all his life and heart problems for several years. He worked for the railway in Ontario but was told by doctors to move west and buy a farm so he could relax. He and my grandmother found a farm in Alberta and raised their children there. Then when he was in his mid-fifties they moved to an acreage near Vancouver, B.C. where they lived for a short time. They had just sold that acreage when he died at fifty-seven years of age from a stroke. I never knew him.

Grandpa had eight siblings. Two died in their sixties from heart attacks, one died from war wounds, three lived into their seventies, one died at eighty, and the age of death of one is unknown. Grandpa's father, my great-grandfather, was fifty-six when he died.

My grandmother, Edna Pearl Relf (nee Robison), lived to be ninety-six. She had three siblings. One died in a car accident in her seventies, one died in her late eighties, and the age the third one died is not known. Both her parents lived to be in their eighties and nineties. According to my generation chart my great-great-great grandfather, James Tuck, lived from 1772 to 1881 and my great-great-great grandmother, Martha Tuck, lived from 1773 to 1883. Both were well over one hundred years-of-age.

Grandma moved to Edmonton after my grandpa died where she worked at various jobs. She ate whatever she wanted all her life. She could finish half a chicken in one meal. Although she stood five foot tall and weighed about 150 pounds, she had a proportioned figure. She said she always felt better a little fleshier.

She wore shoes with about a one inch heel. She never exercised but was active and did a lot of walking even in those heels.

I remember her living on her own in various places as I was growing up and she seemed to have a busy social life. In her early eighties she moved into a lodge which had an eleven o'clock curfew. However, Grandma liked to push the envelope. One evening she stayed out too late and was speeding to get back before the doors were locked. She was pulled over by the police and given a ticket. She had her driving licence until she was eighty-five years of age.

At ninety-one she moved into a nursing care facility where she was put on a diet by her doctor. She hated that but circumvented her doctor by having one of her sons bring her chocolates which she hid in a drawer. She had no immunization during her life and was never sick, not even with the flu. I feel that her good health offset my grandfather's high blood pressure and she gave her children twenty or more years of life because of that.

My grandparents had seven children. The oldest died of lung cancer at age seventy-four. The next four all suffered numerous strokes before dying from strokes in their eighties. The uncle two years older than my mother was ninety-three when he passed away.

My grandparents' youngest child, Frances Olive (my mother), left the home farm near Radway, Alberta, when she was eighteen and went to Vancouver with a friend. They both found work and she met my father when he returned to that city from Europe after World War II. He bought my grandparents acreage and the way he put it was that he bought the acreage and got the daughter for free. They were married for fifty-four years.

My mother maintained her weight all her life. She did have slightly high blood pressure which she controlled by taking the lowest dosage of a blood pressure drug. On it her blood pressure was normal. She also kept her cholesterol in check by taking the smallest dosage of a cholesterol-reducing drug.

Her breakfast consisted of three different high-fibre cereals mixed together with half a banana. She made soups and stews for many of her other meals and liked peanut butter sandwiches. For exercise she line danced once a week, and climbed and descended two flights of stairs eight times an evening, four evenings a week. She also walked the hallways of West Edmonton Mall with Dad or with friends.

Mom lived on her own after my father died until she was eighty-eight and she had her own car up until then. Most Mondays she picked up four friends and they went to the Edmonton Museum to watch the old movies presented there. Afterwards they'd go out for coffee then she'd take everyone to their homes. On the evenings that the movies weren't showing, the ladies went to Mom's place, and they played cards. Every other Tuesday morning she met for lunch with the men and women she had worked with at Sears. Thursday mornings she had Bible study and in the afternoons attended a crafting group.

On the last Wednesday of every month, she attended the Sapper's lunch at the Royal Canadian Legion. My father was a Sapper during WW II and for years until he died they went to the monthly luncheons together. Two or three times a year she took a Mystery Bus Tour with friends. They did not know the destination nor what to expect until they got there. Plus, she travelled to visit family and took holidays. Just before her eighty-seventh birthday she went on a three week European tour with my sister.

She had a very positive attitude and when she wasn't busy with her social life she read or knit lap warmers and shoulder covers for the elderly people in senior's homes.

My grandfather on my dad's side, Joe Donaldson, died at age eight-one of a bowel obstruction. He refused to go to the hospital because as he put it. "They kill you there." This was before I was born.

My grandmother, Sophia, (nee Bouvier) fell and ruptured her spleen at age seventy-six. In those days nothing was done in the way of operating and she died as a result. Although I met my grandmother when I was a baby, I can basically say that I never knew either of them.

They had eleven children. Their youngest died at age twenty-four from a blood clot after an appendix operation. One daughter died at fifty-four from breast cancer. Of the others, two were eighty-one when they died, two were eight-five, then the ages of the others were ninety-one, ninety-two, ninety-three, and ninety-five.

My father, Oliver Hugh, died of complications from prostate cancer at eighty-two. His hair was only slightly gray at the temples and many people thought he was in his late sixties because of his smooth facial skin. Dad was raised on a farm in southern Saskatchewan. During the Depression, he took a prospecting course through the government. He then moved to southern B.C. and spent a few years living on a gold claim with his brothers.

Dad joined the army in 1940 and fought in Italy and Holland. When he returned to Vancouver after the war he met my mother, and they bought my grandparents' acreage. Dad worked for an oil company then he and Mom decided to head to Alberta to farm. Eventually they moved into Edmonton and Dad began working for the railway. He retired after twenty-seven years.

He kept himself in excellent condition, walking in the summer evenings, shovelling snow in winter. He built a house on their lake lot. When he died friends and family said that he had lived a long life, and at the time I believed them, but now I know differently. He was only two-thirds of the way through his life span.

Although there are some health concerns, long life is a fact on both sides of my family. I plan on extending that longevity into the 120s.

I have personally been dealt my genes with their advantages and disadvantages. They impact upon everything about me from my health to how my body works. I had thought, with my family history, that I had found the one aspect in my life that I could count on to help me live long and well, that it was a point in my favour on my way to living to a healthy older age.

Until I read that some doctors at the Mayo Clinic think the influence of genes on our aging has been overrated. They say that only about 20% of what predicts how well I will age is controlled by my genes; that 80% of how I age is based more on whether I smoked, consumed alcohol, lived with constant stress, ate right, and did some physical activity.

At one time it was believed that genes were the one factor of aging that people had no control over, but that idea is changing. My genes are not rigid; what my parents passed on to me in the way of hereditary characteristics, good or bad, are not necessarily what I ended up with. My genes are flexible so I can overcome any family problems and live a healthy life. Conversely, I can take healthy genes given me and inflict my own hardships on them.

My genes respond to what I eat, my stress level, and my emotions. I will age because of aging in my DNA which is the result of free radicals. These are generated by my metabolism and lifestyle. I do have a DNA repair kit that searches for faulty DNA formations but over time it may lose some of its effect.

While I do produce my own antioxidants to combat free radicals, sometimes they may get overpowered by the onslaught of infections, surgery, smoking, and sunlight. If the environment around my genes is kept in good condition, that is, if I eat nutritional foods, keep stress down, exercise, and don't smoke or drink, then my genes will be hearty. And, of course, if I don't look after my genes then they will suffer and so will I.

The best advice I found was to not take anything for granted about longevity. I can have mastery over my health and my aging. I can control what I feed my body, I can control how much exercise I get, I can control the amount of stress I am subjected to and my reaction to it, I can even control the amount of toxins I am exposed to, and I can control how much sleep I get.

I can help my genes. Unfortunately for most of my life I haven't especially when it came to my diet.

Chapter 10
Calorie Restriction Theory

One of the most popular themes in the books on aging is that eating less food was the key to a longer life. When I first read about the calorie restriction theory, I thought it was what I needed to do to live to my maximum life span.

Calories are a way of measuring how much energy a food contains. When food is eaten and absorbed, my body turns those calories into energy to be used for breathing, walking, waving, for any movement it makes. Calories that aren't of immediate use are stored as fat. As most people know, once fat is stored they have to work hard to burn it off.

What I need more of in my diet are high-nutrient, low calorie foods. Eating more calories than my body requires not only causes me to gain weight, it also ages my arteries and immune system, and could induce diabetes and high blood pressure.

Restricting calories is sometimes termed "undernutrition without malnutrition." It means eating just enough food to provide all the essential nutrients but with a lower calorie intake. It doesn't matter whether people cut down on fats, protein, or carbohydrates, so long as all the nutrients are there. It is the reduction in calories that counts. However, if not done right, it could lead to anemia and calcium deficiency.

Food restriction in adults is supposed to increase the number of years the human body lives. One group of people cited in this respect are the Japanese who live on the island of Okinawa. They are reported to eat 20% less food then the regular Japanese population and yet Okinawa has the highest number of centenarians in the world and four times as many as in the rest of Japan.

All of the research has been done on other species such as mice, rats, and monkeys. According to those studies, mice on calorie restricted diets are healthier, perform better in tests of stamina and endurance, and in study groups many of the so-called markers of aging change more slowly. They show a reduced accumulation of oxidative damage from free radicals.

Critics of the plan say that the diet-caused longevity is peculiar to small, short-lived species because they are the ones that most need this flexibility in their life histories. In the study on food deprivation on laboratory rats, one book pointed out that those rats were bred for rapid growth which, in itself, leads to a shorter life span. By restricting their caloric intake, it was causing the rats to live their normal life span. Laboratory rats generally can eat whatever they want while the ones in real life eat only when they find food and they get exercise while looking for that food. Therefore, short rations for rats has been the norm for centuries.

Researchers do wonder if it is the restricted diet that slows aging or the unrestricted one that speeds it up in those animals.

Most gerontologists believe that what works for mice and rats will also work for humans and that dietary restriction is the basis to a longevity program. They state a good time for humans to begin a calorie restricted diet is once we reach eighteen. They also think a reduction of one-third of the calories needed in a normal maintenance diet is what we should strive for. This would depend on a person's job and activity rate.

The more I learned about this theory, the more doubtful I became. The only thing proven in humans is that less food does create a lowered metabolic rate and the body runs at a lower temperature. There is a drop in fasting blood sugar levels and glucose blood levels. Also, the decrease in food intake results in a decrease in free radicals. As for the people on Okinawa, besides eating less food than people in North America, a contributing factor to their length of life could be the main foods in their diet: fish, vegetables, and soy products.

But because I am trying to live to 120 years of age I did cut back on my calories, and I did lose weight. However, I felt I was stressing my body by under eating. I was in a constant state of hunger and my body never seemed to adjust to it. It felt like I was on a diet that would never end. I was tired and listless, a direct contradiction to what I had read. Maybe a lifetime of overeating conditioned my body to expect a certain number of calories and when I didn't provide them, it protested.

But, though it didn't work for me, I found out that frugal eating to extend life is not new. All the books that mentioned calorie restriction also talked about Luigi Cornaro, a Venetian nobleman, who was born in 1468. At the age of forty he was near death, mainly because of his high fat diet and alcohol consumption. (Some articles claim he was thirty-five at the time.) On the advice of his doctors, he changed his eating and drinking habits and became determined to live to the age of one hundred.

He ate sparingly, and generally followed the ancient Greek and Roman notions of a meagre diet being the key to longevity. He limited himself to 340 gm (12 oz) of food and 400 ml (14 oz) of wine each day. Within a year he was in great health.

At the age of eighty-three he composed his first treatise on dieting. He wrote three more at ages eighty-five, eighty-eight, and ninety-five. His two cardinal rules were: eat what agrees with your digestion (quality); and eat as little as possible (quantity). As mentioned in some books and articles he died at ninety-eight and in others he died at 102. But all stated that he remained in possession of his mental and physical faculties until the very end of his life. The average Venetian of Cornaro's day only lived to thirty-five.

But he is the only one who has proven the calorie-restriction theory. I could not find another person who had consciously done the same and documented it.

I did watch a television show where three people were interviewed who were on the Calorie Restriction Diet. One man started ten years earlier while a husband and wife team have been on it for seventeen years. The three began the diet with the sole purpose of trying to live to 120 years-of-age and they all said they have had more energy since beginning it.

I have consciously decided to live to 120 years-of-age, but I will not be doing it by going on the Calorie Restriction Diet.

Chapter 11
Stress and Sleep

Stress is the response my body has to any physical, emotional, or mental demand arising from any given situation. Catabolism is a breakdown of my body's healthy functions, which can take place when I am experiencing a high amount of stress. Anabolism is my body's ability to repair itself. It is a state when my systems are constantly replenishing themselves with new and stronger tissue growth.

My body's reaction to stress is very complex. Once my body senses any type of physical, mental, or emotional threat, my adrenal glands release the hormone cortisol, and my body prepares to do battle or to flee. Within fifteen minutes of continued severe stress and the resulting high levels of cortisol circulating in my blood, my immune system could be so suppressed that it would be unable to impede any enemy that attacked my body.

However, if my mind and body adapt to the stressor, then DHEA is released to level out the cortisol, and everything returns to normal.

Stress is one of the worst, if not the worst, depressors of my immune system. It is a leading cause of diseases among any age group. It contributes to pain and premature aging.

If it does not disappear, my body will go into distress. There are over 150 different symptoms that show my body's inability to adapt to stress. Some of them are high blood pressure, headaches, rapid heartbeat, various aches and pains, muscle tension, difficulty sleeping, concentration problems, addictions, mood swings, and restlessness. My pancreas' response becomes inefficient at reacting to the stimulation and to the cortisol. The key result of this is that there could be an increased resistance to insulin along with a disproportionate release of insulin. This leads to hypoglycemia and eventually burnout of my pancreas. The ultimate disaster could be adult-onset diabetes.

High levels of cortisol are linked to fatigue, insulin resistance, high blood pressure, impotence, osteoporosis, depression, an increase in illness, heart disease, and loss of muscle. All of which are similar to what the scientists say are the diseases and signs of elder age. It also interrupts my body's production of antibodies or may destroy antibodies already in circulation throughout my body.

Negative stress increases my body's production of free radicals, which are a cause of aging and disease. Many people who are under a lot of stress are constantly fighting a cold or some other illness such as bronchitis or pneumonia.

It is hard for me to judge how much actual stress I have suffered during my life because the word "stress" has only shown up in our everyday vocabulary in the past few decades. I knew I had an automatic reaction to any tension-filled condition in my life, but I never realized what that reaction was called and what it was doing to my body.

Like everyone, I have had some stressful times: moving from the city to the country, divorcing, a blended family, deaths. During that first year on the farm when I spent much of my time in solitude I got to know myself very well. I became my close friend and confidant. Since then, I have called upon that intimacy to get me through the bad times. I have helped myself deal with my hurt and sorrow.

Mike's sister, Salliann, was the first one in either of our immediate families to die. I had seen the tragedy of death strike my friends but didn't understand how devastating it could be until it happened to me. On our gold claim I would sit on a large rock beside the river and watch the water flow sedately by. During that time, a deep sense of relaxation settled over me, the first I had felt since the beginning of that turbulent year of wedding plans and watching death approach.

Being beside the calming water helped me deal with the fact that I had witnessed death at work in my family. In the peace and tranquility of our claim I was able to acknowledge that many of the people I loved would probably die before me, though I really didn't want it to ever happen.

I once read on a sign outside a church: "Others see your actions; God knows your thoughts." I wish to take that one step further. "Others see my actions; God, and I, know my thoughts."

I always have known the real reasons why I act the way I do; I know my total thoughts on any situation. Even during the times when I am smiling and saying the right things I give myself full permission to think the opposite. I often have a good laugh with myself over the difference between my actions and my thoughts. And that is okay. I can think what I want. It is not a crime. I am not going to tell on myself.

I believe that knowing myself and accepting myself early in my twenties has kept my mental stress levels from rising too high during parts of my life. I have never lost touch with myself, nor do I ever plan to.

It has been proven that people who experienced a high level stress situation have developed infections or even cancer soon after. I have seriously looked at this statement. I discovered a cancerous lump in my breast four months after my father died. I don't think that it developed during the time since his death, because it wasn't an aggressive type. I believe I had it way before he died, I just didn't find it until after.

I know I was under stress during the three weeks between being told he had terminal cancer and his death. With family coming, taking him to his doctor's and the cancer clinic, and just spending time at my parent's house, I was very busy. After his death I didn't sleep well, one of the signs of stress, so I spent a lot of time playing the game *FreeCell* on my computer, starting at game one. For a while after he died I continued playing, working my way up to game 1000. There were only three games that I couldn't solve. Once I made it to 1000 I was able to quit and get back to my life.

I also told myself that my father's body had picked his time to die. It didn't want him to go through the long, drawn out process of dying from cancer, so it took him out of the game early and quickly.

Some people feel stress occasionally, as many as 33% of North Americans experience stress several times a week, and an unlucky few have stress in their lives that lasts for long periods of time. The World Health Organization says three-quarters of a million people die each year from overwork. In Japan, it is called "Karoshi" which means "death from overwork." An increasing number of workers are suffering, and dying, from cardiovascular diseases because of the stress in their lives.

I feel that "having to have" is one of the biggest stressors of all. During my life I have lived in mobile homes and five bedroom homes. I have driven new sports cars and old clunkers. But I have always hated owing money, so I don't like mortgages or payments, and I avoid them as much as possible. I would rather live in a small home and have it paid off than live in a larger home with a heavy mortgage. I value my freedom from worry.

I have worked at various jobs in my life: bookkeeper, bar cleaner, chamber maid, grocery cashier, bank teller, printing press operator, meat wrapper, shipper, and care giver. But I am not a 9 to 5 type of person. I don't like getting up to an alarm clock so most of those employments only lasted a year or two. The jobs I have held since my children left home have been evening shifts by choice. I like to have my days to myself.

When I was between occupations I wrote. My first article sold when I was thirty-seven. Since then, I have written, and had published, a few historical and travel articles, seven travel books, a short story, six mystery novels, five historical novels, and two holiday romances with my sister, Gwen. The time I spend writing is, and has been, very relaxing but my stress level has always risen when I receive those dreaded rejection slips.

Stress can age me inside and out. Much of my wellness, and therefore my longevity, depends on me. I have to take care of myself, my whole physical, mental, emotional self. I have to think of me first. I have developed a few strategies that I use to help me relax and cope with the adverse aspects of any stress that enters my life.

Over the years, I have realized that I don't have to make everyone's life right; that if they had a problem, it is not up to me to try and solve it.

Every time I remember a negative period in my past, my body relives the stress it felt then. I have to remind myself that I am not back when that happened, that I am living here and now. To do that I have begun to say out loud. "I am not there, I am here." By doing this I can take myself out of that time and bring myself back to the present where I have no stress

I have tried relaxation techniques, such as deep breathing and just slowing down. I find these are one of the best methods to relieve my stress, which in turn keeps my blood pressure down, improves my immune system, and generally helps me age better.

I make an effort to be cheerful and happy, to enjoy people, to get outdoors and into my yard, and mainly to reinforce my good thoughts of myself.

I deal with any anger I feel for I know it can upset my whole body and take over my life. I ask myself if this is important in my life and will it make any difference to me tomorrow.

I have never liked arguments and I try to avoid them as much as possible. When I do get into one I take the time to decide if it is worth the effort. Does it really matter who wins? Will I remember the argument tomorrow? Will I even remember who won? Sometimes it is just easier to agree and carry on with my life since the stress I am under is usually more critical than what the argument is about.

I have decided that if something unfortunate happens it is okay to take the time, from an hour or two to a few days, depending on what it is, to feel sorry for myself. But then I have to deal with it and get going again. My life continues.

I think of my mental comfort when I buy things as much as I do of my physical comfort. I know that a high standard of living with its stresses does not equate with a good quality of life. I have reached that stage in my life where I have quit playing the buying game, where I know that having lots of possessions isn't important.

I love to laugh. Laughter relieves stress and enables me to let go of any angry feelings I have. It boosts the release of endorphins, my body's natural painkiller, and suppresses my stress hormones.

Forgiveness, whether of myself or others, is another great stress reliever. Holding onto anger, bitterness, and resentment puts my body into stress mode. I do not assign blame any more.

My stress level is very low now. I have a good husband, good family, and good friends. I am retired. I write. I talk with, or text, my children often and see them and my grandchildren and great-grandchildren when I can.

I am glad that I am at the age where I can relax; where I don't force deadlines on myself or have them forced upon me. I watch younger people hurrying through their lives, their stress building. I want to tell them it is not necessary. But I know they will not listen, for I, too, thought I had to do the same at that age.

Oh, what a wonderful feeling it is to have most of the stress of life lifted, to be at this perfect age. Right now, in my seventies, my life is good.

Some of the centenarians and supercentenarians I read about stated that they tended not to dwell on things. They manage their stress rather than let their stress manage them.

So, living a long life has a lot to do with not worrying too much.

* * *

One of the most neglected factors in health and longevity is sleep, both in terms of length and quality. Sleep has not always been understood by the medical sector. They used to say that sleep overcame sleepiness and that lack of sleep caused sleepiness. But sleep studies by the U.S. Department of Health have found that the proper amount of sleep is very necessary to healthy living.

During sleep my cell growth and tissue repair are faster. Growth hormone, also known as the youth hormone, and the hormone melatonin, which benefits my immune system, are released while I sleep.

Not only does my body require sleep, but so does my brain. It needs to rest after a full day's work, so it is able to commit the information it gathered during the day to long-term memory. I perform better mentally and physically at anything I do if I have had enough sleep.

People today sleep less than our ancestors did one hundred years ago. In the late 1700s the average North American got ten hours of sleep each night. People went to bed when it turned dark and rose at day light. Did the Industrial Revolution disconnect us from that natural sleep cycle? Was that when we began to ignore our ancestor's years of evolutionary adaptability?

The amount of sleep I require has not been constant during my lifetime. I needed up to twenty hours a day when I was a baby, then the number began to decline as I grew older and had more to do in my life.

Today many people, for various reasons, get about five hours of sleep. They watch too much television or are on their computers or cell phones. They think they will miss something if they go to bed. If there is an undertaking they feel they must do they will fit it into their schedules even if it means giving up sleep time. Some even think that going to bed on time is a sign of a boring life. All these are choices everyone makes.

Although it is thought that seven to eight hours of sleep a night is sufficient, I find I sometimes need more than that to really feel rested. A John Hopkins study showed that having an hour power nap in the afternoon can keep people more alert, and give them more patience and efficiency, better health and reaction time, and less stress. For me, ten to twenty minutes works well.

The medical sector now knows that not getting enough sleep is a stressor to my body. When I worked, one of my jobs included working a rotation of day, afternoon, evening, and graveyard shifts over a period of weeks. I didn't like getting up and being at work at eight in the morning for the day shift. The afternoon and evening shifts, which started at four o'clock, were my favourites because I could sleep in until I was rested, and I had much of my day to myself. The afternoon shift ended at nine o'clock, the evening at midnight.

Although, there were only four graveyard shifts at a time, they were very hard on me. I was not able to fall asleep when I got home just after eight o'clock in the morning. Everyone else in the neighbourhood was getting up and ready for work and the noise level was high. It would take about an hour or so for things to quiet down and I would go to bed. But there was always the person who would phone, or someone would decide to mow his lawn, or just normal traffic on the road would wake me. Plus, my body just didn't feel right going to sleep when the sun was up.

Even though I would get around six hours sleep during the day, it was not enough. By the third day I would be grumpy and groggy. On the fourth I would sleep a couple of hours then try to stay up until evening so that I could get my sleep pattern back to normal because in two days I would be on day shift again. It was a tough schedule, and I was glad when I applied for and got a straight afternoon shift.

In 2008, the International Agency for Research on Cancer, a section of the World Health Organization, decided to add working the graveyard shift to the list of "probable" causes of cancer. And it is based on statistics that show a higher rate of breast and prostate cancer among women and men who work during the hours between sunset and sunrise.

Luckily, my time working graveyards was short.

Part Three

The Effect of Aging on the Systems and Organs of My Body

Chapter 12

Changes to My Body as I Grow Older

I was amazed to learn the number of changes that supposedly have already taken place in my body and the ones that supposedly will take place as I age. Not all of the deteriorations stated occur in everyone, and if they do, it is not at the same rate. Some people don't show any of the aging signs while others can hardly move for all their ailments. The reasons could be genetics, lifestyle, or luck, or a bit of all three. I have prepared a list of some of the changes that I read could occur or have occurred in my body as I age.

There will be a slow deterioration in the activity of enzymes, beginning at about the age of thirty-five and continuing at an increasing rate thereafter.

My blood pressure and cholesterol levels may rise.

Abnormal proteins may increase in my blood, such as the rheumatoid factor, considered a cause of arthritic joint inflammation.

I may lose height by up to 5 cm (2 in). Men could be shorter by up to 6.3 cm (2.5 in).

My ear lobes will lengthen, bags may form below my eyes, my cheek and jowl skin could begin to sag, and my nose might become wider and longer.

A fluctuation in my body water could lead to problems with dehydration.

By the time I reached the age of seventy, the blood flow to my brain, my kidney filtration rate, my resting heart output, my lung volume during exercise, my body water content, my metabolism, and my brain weight may all have decreased between 20 and 60%.

I am past that seventy age mark. My blood pressure fluctuates between 110/70 and 120/80, the same that it has been all my life. I don't have arthritic joint inflammation, my resting heart is the same as it was twenty years ago (62), I haven't noticed any change in my lung volume, and my height is the same. I don't have bags under my eyes, but my jowl skin is sagging a little. I can't tell if my lobes are longer, but I think my nose is larger.

Cells are the building blocks of my tissues, and my body has trillions of different types of cells. Each cell, with the exception of red blood cells, is a complete unit that has its own DNA. Red blood cells don't have DNA and only survive a few months before being destroyed and replaced.

Some of my body cells, called mitotic, divide up to fifty times before dying. These cells are found in my gastrointestinal tract, my skin, the lymphocytes of my immune system, and in the red and white cells in my blood. Other cells, called postmitotic, cease dividing once the body part they are forming has reached maturity. They are in my brain, my nerves, and my muscles.

A third type falls between these two, stopping their division but restarting again when necessary. Evidence of this is my liver, which if damaged or partially cut away, will regenerate.

There is normal cell death occurring in my body every day, and some of it is to keep my body operating at peak efficiency. Some cells wear out and are replaced. Others die and are not replaced. Part of this cell death is initiated by my body, such as the cells in my immune system that kill themselves to keep an invading virus from dividing inside them and spreading. Some cells are instructed by other nearby cells to destroy themselves if they are in danger of becoming cancerous.

All cells become larger with age and their ability to divide and reproduce lessens. Connective tissue may stiffen making the vessels, organs, and airways more rigid. These changes in the tissues can cause alterations to the organs. However, they may not always be seen because most people don't continually use their organs to their full capacity.

When the cells of an organ fail, that organ fails. If a person has heart failure, kidney failure, or failing eyesight it is because the organ is losing its ability to effectively do its work. It means that too many cells of the organ have died or are not functioning properly.

Because I really don't feel any different in my seventies than I have at any other age, I guess these deteriorations haven't had much influence on my body. However, I can wait and see if they will affect me in the future or I can work at minimizing the effects of those changes in my body. The choice is mine to make.

Chapter 13

My Immune System

When I was a teenager people always thought I was in my twenties. Throughout my thirties, forties and fifties, people never believed me when I told them my age or how old my children were, or that I had grandchildren or great-grandchildren. I would always get: "You don't look old enough to have children that age." "You don't look old enough to have grandchildren." "You don't look fifty-seven or sixty or seventy."

Even now, when I say my youngest grandchild is in her late-twenties, people don't believe it. I always feel good after someone tells me I don't look my age. My ego has been stroked. But the stickler is that what they are basing my age on is how old my face looks. Not on how well my body moves or how healthy it is under my skin. I know it is not my face nor compliments that will determine how well I age. It is how I treat my body and my mind that will make the difference.

My immune system consists of the thymus gland, bone marrow, antibodies, and a trillion white blood cells. If I didn't have an immune system I would quickly die due to the onslaught of lethal viruses and cancer cells. One of my immune system's jobs is to identify the millions of infectious microbes, antigens (viruses, fungi, bacteria, toxins, and foreign blood cells), and anything else that attacks my body each day as well as detect my own cells that have turned cancerous. Another of its jobs is to destroy and remove all those invaders and cells.

Unfortunately, my immune system is one of the first systems that may degenerate as I age. According to the books, by the time I reached my forties, the thymus gland, the master gland of my immune system, had shrunk to about 10 to 15% of the size it was when I was aged eleven.

Genes, luck, exercise, and eating a nutritional diet do play a big part in me having a strong immune system, but there are many outside culprits that could weaken my ability to fight off illness and disease. Emotional stress is believed by many researchers to be the most powerful single inhibitor of our immune system. Others think it is cigarettes and smoking.

Some immune suppressors may include: food laden with sugar or fats, prolonged exposure to electrical devices, breathing polluted air, sedentary living, being overweight, not getting enough sleep, certain drugs, and too much alcohol.

My immune system is controlled by the same genes that guide my aging process. When it gets to the point where it cannot clean my body of defective and dead normal cells, the resulting buildup of garbage will be hard on my organs and they, too, could begin to age. My immune system may also lose its ability to destroy and remove outside organisms that invade my body. Heart disease, arthritis, cancer, and pneumonia are some of the problems that may occur if my immune system begins to lose potency.

My mental and physical health also makes a large difference in how my immune system fights off attackers. My mind and body are so connected that my immune system even responds to my mood. Negative or destructive thoughts and feelings can suppress it; while thinking and feeling positive about myself and my body increases my immunity.

The year 2016 started out normal for me. I was working on two books, a young adult Canadian historical novel, *West to Grande Portage,* and a holiday romance titled, *Twelve Dates of Christmas*, with my sister, Gwen, which had to be done by the middle of August in order to be published in October. Then in February of that year my publisher decided to put together a series of books titled Canadian Historical Brides to come out the end of 2016 and into 2017 to celebrate Canada's 150th birthday. She wanted the first one to be published in September and the others to be published at two month intervals. She asked her Canadian writers to choose a province or territory and when they thought they could have the book completed. I picked the Yukon and decided that I could have it done by April of 2017. I was also working twenty hours a week so I figured that would give me time to finish the young adult and holiday romance.

I completed the young adult in March of 2016 and sent it to my publisher. It came out in May. My summer started fine. Gwen and I were working on our holiday romance, and I was starting research on my Yukon book, which I titled *Romancing the Klondike*. Then my publisher asked if I could have my Yukon novel ready by October of 2016. I knew when the story was taking place and some of the characters so I thought I could manage it and agreed.

But I didn't realize the stress it would put on me.

I spent all my time writing. I didn't get to relax on my deck with my husband, I didn't get to walk on our boardwalk through the trees in our back yard, I didn't get to sleep in on my days off, I didn't clean the house. As time went on I quit worrying about my diet, eating what was available and as much as I wanted. I drank a lot of cola. I cut back on my exercises, only doing them once or twice a week. I began to gain weight. I lost sleep. I became sedentary, sitting most of my days at the computer.

But the writing was getting done.

My mother's birthday was in August and, as usual, I planned the party. I travelled from where I lived in Port Alberni, on Vancouver Island, to Red Deer, Alberta, to celebrate with Mom and my family and then was a panelist at a writer's conference in Calgary the next weekend. Back at home, Gwen and I did a final read-through of our novel and sent it off. I finished my Yukon book and also emailed it. When *Twelve Dates of Christmas* came back from the editors, I made the corrections and returned it.

But Mom's health was going downhill. I went back to Alberta and spent three weeks visiting her every day. All four of us children made it to Red Deer for Thanksgiving. During that time my *Romancing the Klondike* manuscript came back from the editors, and I worked on it then sent it back.

After Thanksgiving I returned home. My husband, Mike, had kidney stones and wasn't well. He was scheduled for an operation in November. I went back to work. I received *Romancing the Klondike* manuscript for the final edit, and I returned to work. Again, I was under pressure, although the publishing date had been set back to January. Then one day my sister-in-law called and said that Mom had been moved to hospice. I was torn between staying with my husband during his operation or going to be with Mom. Mike insisted I go, and I arrived at the hospice Friday night. Mom died Saturday night.

Mike had his operation on the same day and roughly the same time that we were having Mom's funeral service.

When I got back home a week and a half after the funeral, Mike was not well. The doctor had put in a ureter stent, and it was painful plus he had kidney infection. Christmas was coming and we were expecting company, so I began to prepare by going out and buying bags of chocolates and eating them. I'd already gained weight over the summer and fall so as far as I was concerned, it didn't matter. To me, eating and Christmas went together.

But some of the stress was of my own making because I am a perfectionist. My publisher would have changed dates for me if I'd asked but I had stated I would have those books done and I was not stopping until they were all written.

Our Christmas company arrived with a cold and when they left, Mike was coming down with it. I've always prided myself that my immune system was strong. And, for a while, it was. It was two weeks before I began to feel sick. I came down with a bad cold: coughing, stuffed head, runny nose. I even missed a couple of days' work.

I now know that the stress of writing my books, losing my mother (bereavement can raise the cortisol level in a person's body for up to six months), and worry about my husband's health lowered my immunity so that I caught the cold. I had been drinking a lot of pop and eating a lot of chocolates and other sweets before and during the holidays which also fostered my cold. Really, how much can an immune system take?

After all the years of reading and learning and trying to do right, it finally sank in what my overeating and pop drinking was doing to my body. I cut back on both of them.

While our immune system is the great defender of our body, sometimes it can get out of control. In some people the immune system cells begin producing autoantibodies that target their own blood vessels, nerves, and other normal cells. Their body then begins attacking itself and some of the diseases that can develop are diabetes, multiple sclerosis, lupus, ulcerative colitis, and rheumatoid arthritis.

I have Vitiligo, which is the loss of melanin, the pigment that gives my skin its colour. Vitiligo presents as white patches on the skin and is due to the destruction of the pigment-forming cells called melanocyctes. It affects about 1% of the world's population and is found in all skin colours although it is more conspicuous in people with darker skin.

The exact cause of Vitiligo is not known but some doctors believe it is an autoimmune disease where certain white cells of the immune system kill the melanocycte cells. I don't know if I believe this since I am very healthy otherwise. I have also been told it is hereditary, is attributable to stress, and could be caused by physical trauma or sunburn. One doctor I saw said it was due to a change in hormones from giving birth.

The condition usually develops before people reach the age of forty. I was about thirty-five when I first noticed itchy, lighter sections on my neck. Then parts of the backs of my hands stayed white when I tanned. Since I tanned quite dark, some people thought I had a terrible disease.

I did observe that it formed roughly the same shape and size on each side of my body. Both sides of my neck had the same kind of white patch, as did my hands. Over the years it slowly spread to more of my body.

I have to stay out of the sun because my skin burns instantly. Even on hot, sunny days when I want to work in the yard or garden, I wear long sleeves, long pants, gloves, a large hat, socks, and shoes.

It is not harmful to my health and there is no cure. Some treatments recommended are de-pigmenting the remaining skin, using dyes on the affected skin, cosmetics, rubbing on corticosteroid creams, and skin grafting. When I was first diagnosed I was told I could start on a drug that would stop the progression of the white patches, but I would have to take it for the rest of my life. I do not like to take drugs of any sort, so I refused. I am without pigment over about 75% of my body.

Since reading about my immune system and all that can attack it, I have scrutinized my own history of illness. In spite of all that can go wrong with it, one good thing about my immune system is that it retains its memory. As I experienced colds and the flu during my early life I developed immunity to those strains of viruses and that has allowed my body to fight off any infections I have already been exposed to.

My personal choice is not to have flu shots. In the past thirty years I have had the shots twice for work purposes only. I have not had the flu in those thirty years, and I cannot remember when I actually did have it last.

I am happy to say that my immune system is strong and working well for me. During the Covid pandemic I took the usual precautions of wearing a mask and using hand sanitizer when I went out shopping. I had my two shots and three boosters and thankfully never got the disease. When the restrictions were lifted, I went back to my normal way of life.

And the good news is that as I continue to age I should not develop infections if I continue to have a healthy immune system.

Chapter 14
My Skin, Hair, and Nails

It was an eye opener to learn that my skin, hair, and nails were all part of the same group, that my skin has the ability to change its collagen molecules into hair and nails.

My skin is the single largest organ of my body. It regulates my temperature and hydration and protects the inside of my body from the extreme temperatures, pollutants, and sun rays of my environment. My skin scrutinizes everything around me through its pain, touch, and temperature receptors and then sends the gathered information to my brain for analysis.

There are two layers of skin called the dermis or inner layer and the epidermis or outer layer. The thickness of the epidermis varies. It is 0.05mm on my eyelids and 1.5mm on my palms and the soles of my feet. The dermis has oil glands, nerve fibres, sweat glands, immune and fat cells, and many kilometres of blood vessels. Below the dermis is water and collagen, which is a protein. The collagen binds to the water and fills out my skin while allowing it to fold and stretch as I move. Aging causes the collagen to become stiff and drier and it begins to crease instead of snapping back into place. Those creases become the wrinkles in my skin.

The cells of my dermis divide to form a new layer of skin which rises to the top. The older layer flakes off so that my skin is renewed every twelve months.

Before my vitiligo, my face was seldom covered. It was exposed to sunlight along with much of the rest of my body in the summer and open to the cold and the wind and the snow of winter.

This part of my body that is bared to all the elements, is also the part that society has labelled as the foremost indicator of my aging. And like everyone else I am judged by the wrinkles around my eyes and mouth and on my cheeks, and as these increase, I could be deemed old, useless, and no longer attractive.

Maybe having to stay out of the sun since my thirties has helped save my skin from early aging.

The skin all over my body began losing elasticity when I was in my twenties. As I grew older there was also a decrease in thickness and pigment, and a reduction in the number of sweat glands, in the blood flow to my skin, and in its ability to replace cells. The most noticeable aspect of skin aging is the thinning of the outer layers which causes it to sag.

But, and this is significant, none of these are harmful to my health. No one has ever died from wrinkles or sagging skin.

Smoking ages the skin faster than anything else by increasing the depth and severity of wrinkles, the poor quality of skin texture, and the amount of excess skin.

While the sun can be harmful to my skin it is also a good source of Vitamin D. However, fifteen to twenty minutes of sun exposure three to four times a week is about all I need to get my supply of Vitamin D. After that the ultraviolet light from the sun can cause premature aging to my skin, cataracts to my eyes, and the lethal skin cancer called malignant melanoma.

My skin may lose its elasticity as I age and be slower at healing, but the good news is that it will never wear out.

Hair is a protein strand that grows through an opening or follicle in my skin. Each strand lives between four and five years, then dies. Usually, a new one replaces it. Hair follicles produce a pigment, melanin, which gives my hair its colour.

The amount of hair I have is determined by my genes. Most people suffer hair loss as the rate of hair replacement and growth slows. Both sexes may experience some baldness. Some body hair begins to disappear and what is left is coarser. Men may notice an increase in the hair of their ears, eyebrows, and nose, while women might see hair on their chins and round their lips.

Aging may cause my nails to grow slower and become dull and brittle. Some may turn yellow, opaque, and thicken. Again, though, this doesn't happen to all people.

Other than having Vitiligo, I have no problems with my skin. My nails are thick, strong, and have no discolouration. When I had breast cancer and went on chemotherapy, I opted for a lesser dose over a longer period of time. I was told that my hair would thin out, but I wouldn't lose it all. I was also assured that my hair would fill in again afterwards. Well, not all of it did. The crown of my head now has a lot less hair than it did before treatment.

Chapter 15

My Skeleton and Joints

Being stooped and walking slowly are two of the universal signs of an elder person. My grade one teacher, Mrs. Lee, was bent over and had a hump on her back. Since I was six years old, at the time I just figured it was because she was what I considered to be ancient. Now I know she probably had osteoporosis even though she was only in her early fifties.

My skeleton provides support and structure for my body. The major components of my bones are calcium, phosphorus, and a protein called collagen. Calcium is the most important. Without a certain amount ingested every day, my bones suffer a loss.

My skeleton is constantly renewing itself. As calcium is needed elsewhere in my body one set of cells eat away at my bones forming grooves or indentations. When my blood delivers new calcium to my bones another set of cells fill in the holes with new bone mineral.

There are two major types of bones: cortical, which is the continuous material that makes up the long bones of my body; and trabecular, a fine mesh found inside the vertebrae and at the ends of the hip bones. Both types lose mass, but the trabecular bones suffer the worst effect. This is because they are very thin in all persons of every age so, as a person gets older, these bones can even disappear. This is why people lose height over time.

Total bone mass in some people after the age of thirty decreases by about 1% per year. This leads to an increased risk of osteoporosis and bone breakage. Osteoporosis or bone frailty is a plight among elder people. It is caused by the reduced ability of the bone cells to maintain and remodel the skeleton. As some people age their bones become brittle due to a reduction in bone tissue and density, and a depletion of minerals essential to continued bone formation like phosphorus and calcium.

Women are more prone to bone loss than men and that is because women have less bone to lose. Bone thinning will cause the vertebrae to collapse in one out of three women over the age of sixty-five. By age ninety, one in three women and one in six men will have suffered a hip fracture. Some will mend but for others this could either cause a permanent impairment of mobility or eventual death.

Lack of use tells my body that it doesn't need the bone mass anymore and the replacement of bone tissue slows. My bones may become porous, brittle, and could fracture easily. My wrists, hips, and the vertebrae in my spine are the most common injury sites. A sedentary lifestyle at any age could accelerate these problems.

Bone metabolism never quits, and my bones are capable of growing with use. Every time a bone is moved it bends slightly, which triggers electrical and biochemical changes that stimulate bone formation. As more force is applied, the bending increases and that accelerates the establishment of new bone. As I move, I keep my bone density constant, but additional movement, like weight bearing exercise can help reinforce my bone mass.

I first had my bone density checked when I was fifty and I was told they were denser than normal. The next time was seven years later, and I was still in the high normal range. I drink a lot of milk and eat yogurt, and exercise so this must be helping.

One of the fastest aging parts of my body is my spine. Lower back pain is a major cause of physical disability. About 80% of all back pain is caused by poorly conditioned muscles. I know that it is important to keep my stomach and back muscles flexible and strong by exercising.

I have been lucky in that I haven't worked in jobs that abused my body. I have, on two occasions though, had back problems. The first time I felt back pain was when I was working as a cleaner in a bar and had to move the heavy metal tables. One day my back hurt but I ignored it. It was the same the next day and continued until one day I could barely move. I had to quit that job but continued to work as a part-time chamber maid and a bookkeeper in the hotel. When I finally went to a chiropractor, he told me that my trouble probably went back to when I lived on the farm and carried heavy pails of grain and water to the animals while being pregnant. He was very good, and it wasn't long before I was walking without pain again.

Then, about ten years later I fell while walking my dogs. The first day afterwards I was fine but the second day I could barely get out of bed. By this time, I had moved to a new town. I tried a different chiropractor but for some reason he couldn't correct my problem. I finally made a trip to see my old chiropractor and after just two visits my back was, once more, normal.

Having a sore back totally played havoc with my life. It hurt to stand, it hurt to sit, it hurt to lie down. I even tried lying on the floor with my legs up on the couch, but I couldn't get comfortable. It was a terrible time because I could not do anything without pain.

One of the hardest things on a back is to bend forward unsupported. I decided to itemize the times I bend over in a day. Here is a partial list: making my bed; getting food off the lower levels of the refrigerator; getting something from the lower shelves or bottom drawers of cupboards; putting dishes in the dishwasher; vacuuming; washing floors; putting clothes in and taking them out of the dryer; picking something up off the floor; gardening and raking leaves. These are just around my home, and I didn't do most of them just once. It's no wonder so many people have some sort of problems with their back.

Carrying heavy bags on my shoulders or in one hand is also very hard on my back. I watched an interview of people on the street where they were asked what they carried in their purses or briefcases. Some of the items were: mail; battery charger; books; lots of change in the way of coins; laptops; gym clothes, change of clothes, and shoes. Bags are getting bigger and heavier because of all the stuff that is deemed important to have with us and that puts everyone's backs at risk. I have downsized my purse and only carry heavy bags when necessary and for a short distance.

I find that massage is good for my lower back. If I have been doing a lot of bending over or lifting, I rub my lower back quite often to relax the muscles and I lean backwards working my muscles in the opposite direction. When doing chores around my house or yard I am careful not to bend and twist at the same time. Also, when I sit at my desk while writing, I get up often and walk around to relieve the pressure on my back.

I am certainly vigilant of how I use my back now because growing older with a sore back is not part of my plan for my next forty plus years.

Joints link one bone to another so I can move at the point of connection. They are made up of ligaments and cartilage with a fluid to keep them lubricated. My shoulder, hip, and knee are my most important joints. My shoulder has the greatest mobility, and, because of its wide range of motion, these joints are prone to dislocating.

My hip joint is where many muscles and tendons meet, and it is the most stable. It carries my body weight and usually breaks down from general wear and tear because of constant movement. It will fracture rather than dislocate.

I can harm my knee joints by overuse or by squatting for a long period of time, which puts a strain on them. It is easier on those joints to carry a lighter load so if I gain even 4.5 kg. (10 lbs) in weight, it will feel like almost 14 kg (30 lbs) to my knees. If I walk up or down stairs that same 4.5 kg could increase by seven times so that it is 32 kg (70 lbs) to my knees.

Aging could be the reason for fluid changes, fraying of my cartilage, decreases in the elasticity of my cartilage, and for stiffening of my ligaments. These may cause bone fractures, a shortening of stature, a reduction in flexibility and joint stability, and swelling and pain in my joints.

Hip and knee-replacement surgeries have increased dramatically in Canada since the mid-1990s. As many as 90% of the surgeries are on people aged fifty-five and older, who may have been abusing their joints for years.

So far I have no pain in any of my joints, but I do have to be careful of my knees. While working on my travel book *Backroads of the Yukon and Alaska*, my husband, Mike, and I hiked the Chilkoot Trail. This was in 1997, one hundred years after the Klondikers made their trek to the Klondike gold fields. I carried a backpack that held between 11-14 kg (25-30 lbs) plus I had cameras and a tape recorder dangling from a belt around my waist.

My right knee began to bother me after the first day. It was fine if I was climbing up hill or walking flat but as soon as I started going downhill the extra weight of my pack, added to the force of my body, caused a lot of pain in my joint. I had to wrap it with the two tensor bandages we had brought with us.

This worked fine until the afternoon of the next day when my left knee began to bother me. I moved one bandage to that knee but, alone, neither was supportive enough. The pain slowed me down.

Finally, Mike dug out a pair of his used, elastic support socks from his pack. He wrapped them around the bandages and strapped them in place with black electrical tape he had brought with him. My knees were quite a sight with the tan bandages, the gray socks, and then the shiny black tape. One woman even crossed the campsite to find out where I had bought my unusual knee braces. She smiled slightly and left when I told her what they were.

My pace picked up for the rest of the hike, not only because my knees didn't hurt, but because I had to keep ahead of the odour that wafted up from the socks. That experience enforced in me the damage that added body weight could do to my knees.

I have mistreated my right ankle in some way just about every decade of my life. In my teens I sprained it playing baseball. In my twenties I came down wrong on my right foot during a volleyball game and dislocated my ankle.

A week before Mike and I were to head out on vacation I stepped on a large bone our dog had left on the porch and sprained it again. So, at the age of thirty-eight, I limped through much of our first trip to the Yukon and Alaska.

In my early forties I worked as a shipper in a large warehouse. The driver of one of the motorized pallet jacks lost control of it and ran it into my ankle. I wore a cast for a week and a half then had it removed to attend my daughter's wedding in Las Vegas. My fifties were no better, I stepped on something in the dark while walking my dog along a railway track and sprained it again. It was a long, slow walk home. In my sixties, I was hiking part of the Appalachian Trail in Connecticut with my grandson when I stepped on part of a rock sticking out of the ground and twisted my ankle. I had to walk 8km (5 miles) on the ankle to where my husband waited for us in our motorhome.

So far, in my seventies, I have not harmed it in any way, and I am happy to say that, while I have had some accidents over the years, I have never broken a bone.

Chapter 16
My Senses

Not only do I want to age with a healthy body and mind I also want all my senses to be working. My senses absorb information from the world around me then send that information as a nerve pulse to my brain where it is interpreted into sensations. As I age some of my senses may become less acute. Changes in hearing and eyesight will be the most traumatic for me to handle. I don't want to go blind or deaf or even lose my taste, any of which will affect my enjoyment of my elder years.

I wore glasses for near sightedness from the time I was about age twelve until age fifty. I did not have astigmatism or any other problems so at that age I had lazar surgery done on my eyes. My eyes came out 20/20 after the procedure and they still are. However, I now have what the medical establishment tastefully terms as 'old age' eyes and I do need reading glasses. I still smile that for almost forty years I could see objects and read print up close but not far away. Now, I can see things at a distance, but I need glasses for reading print and looking at things up close.

While I now have perfect vision, I still go for an eye check-up yearly. I want to avoid any problems that can develop which I might not notice but which can be detected by an eye exam. Those problems could include slower adjustment time to darkness, changes in colour perception, and my eye lens could become clouded through the formation of cataracts.

On my last visit to the optometrist, I was told I have the very, very early stages of cataracts. I was advised that if I wear polarized sunglasses that keep out UVA, UVB, and UVC rays every time I go outside I shouldn't have to worry about them getting worse for fifteen or more years. I now carry a pair of those sunglasses with me everywhere I go.

Also, I don't have any signs of glaucoma or macular degeneration, two of the leading causes of eye troubles or blindness I have to watch for as I age.

A clear fluid, called aqueous humor, is produced in the rear chamber of the eye. It flows through the pupil to the front chamber and is drained by way of canals. The cells of the optic nerve may be harmed when the fluid can't drain and puts pressure on the nerve. This raised pressure is known as glaucoma and may eventually cause blindness.

Also, the cells of the retina could become damaged or lost in a condition known as age-related macular degeneration. When I was travelling through Alberta working on my back roads books I met a man at one of the tourist information centres. We began chatting and he told me a bit about his life. He'd been married for forty-three years, and he and his wife had always liked to travel. However, they were now housebound because his wife had macular degeneration. I had never heard of it, so he explained it to me.

The centre of the retina is called the macula and is the most active part of the eye. Macular degeneration is not caused as much from genes as it is from lifestyle and it comes in two forms, wet and dry. The most common one is the dry where there is a loss of the cones and rods in the central part of the eye which results in blindness. There is no known cause or treatment for it, but the people usually affected are those who smoke or have high blood pressure or both. It is the most widespread cause of vision problems in the elderly.

Wet degeneration occurs when abnormal blood vessels, which form under the eye, begin to leak blood elements and damage the retina.

He ended by saying. "It's as if our lives have been cut short."

I have since learned that keeping my arteries clean and elastic will reduce my chances of developing either type of macular degeneration.

Contrary to popular belief, only about 20% of elder people have bad enough vision to impair driving and only about 5% are unable to read. People in their eighties, nineties and even over one hundred still read books with just reading glasses.

I knew a woman who was ninety-nine years old, and her children were always taking her books to read.

I have never worked around loud machinery nor listened to booming music. For a few years I went hunting with my husband and so have been around gunshots. Plus, I have been in the centre of a screaming crowd at hockey or football game. But those were only infrequent times in my life, so my hearing is excellent. Sometimes, though, it is too sensitive. I have had to leave stores and restaurants because I find the music too loud. Mike turns up the volume on our telephone receiver so he can better hear the other person speaking and I always turn it down. I must have inherited my hearing from my mother because hers was also very good.

Normal hearing allows me to select the sounds I want to listen to, such as a conversation I am having with someone in the midst of a crowded room, while screening out the other background noise. The ability to hear involves bones, joints, skin, muscles, nerves, tissue elasticity, and blood supply. When sound hits my eardrum it causes a vibration. This goes to the bones of my middle ear and then to the liquid of my inner ear. There it stimulates nerve cells that connect with the auditory centres of my brain. If any part of this process goes wrong, it will affect my hearing. The gradual loss of my 'hair' cells, that turn the vibration into nerve impulses, and skin changes in my outer ear will be the main causes if I experience hearing loss as I age.

For a few, early hearing loss may occur if they have listened to or worked around loud sounds for an extended period of time. The decibel scale measures the strength of noises and the damage they can do to the ear. Near total silence is zero decibels. Any sound above eighty-five decibels, such as snoring can bring about some hearing loss. Listening to anything over ninety (lawn mower) can generate damage after just two hours, while attending a concert where the decibels reach 110, can result in some permanent hearing loss in less than an hour.

More than one third of elder adults have some sort of hearing loss. Hearing aids do help make voices louder, but they don't necessarily make them clearer.

Touch is the first sense to develop and is the only sense I use for physical contact with my world. The others are all through perception. I use my fingers and hands to identify objects. There are about 100 receptors for touch per square centimetre in my fingertips compared to twenty-five to thirty in my palms and much less on the rest of my body. The sense of touch includes recognition of pain and vibrations.

Not only do I have receptors in my skin to detect temperature, contact, or pain, there are also receptors in my muscles, joints, tendons, and internal organs. Aging may reduce or change some of these sensations, and this reduction or change could increase the risk of injuries from extremes in heat and cold temperatures.

The sense of taste developed early in the human species' evolution to prevent our ancestors from poisoning ourselves as they learned about foods in their environment. I have approximately 5000 taste buds that are not only on my tongue, but on my cheeks, the roof of my mouth, and in my throat as well. Taste buds are made of receptors that can sense the sweet, sour, bitter, and salty tastes in the foods and liquids I consume and process it into a signal for my brain. The tip of my tongue senses sweetness, those on the sides of my tongue react to salty and sour, while the bitter sensation comes from the back of my tongue as well as on my soft palate.

Scientists believe that there is a reason for those senses. Sweet ensures that I will eat foods that supply energy and nutrition; salt maintains my body's fluids and electrolytes balance; sour lets me know foods are spoiled; and bitter warns against toxins and poisons.

We do lose taste buds as we age but for most people there is no loss of sensitivity to the four taste sensations.

Like my hearing my sense of smell is very acute. I sometimes find shopping in some stores hard because of the odours from their products. One time I was driven from a store because of an overwhelming astringent, rubberish smell that must have come from some a new display just set up. It filled the whole store and soon my nose was burning, and I was getting a headache. I only managed a quick look for what I had come for then I had to leave. What surprised me was that no one else seemed to be bothered by it. The staff acted normal, and the customers I saw weren't in any hurry to get out of there.

Much of what I taste is first associated with odours. These come to me through my sense of smell which begins in cells and nerve receptors high in my nose. When odourants enter my nose they go up and bind with the receptors. These receptors then stimulate the nerves below them and those nerves send messages to my brain. Different odourants bind to different receptors, or combinations of receptors, to give the various smells I experience.

While I am capable of identifying and distinguishing about 10,000 different odours, I am not able to detect all smells. If I didn't have certain scents in my surroundings during my formative years I may not be able to recognize them later in my life. But my sense of smell can be trained as shown by perfumers who make a living testing different and new scents.

There is disagreement over whether losing some of our sense of smell and taste is part of normal aging or if it is from diseases, smoking, or environmental toxins. For some who do lose sensitivity in their smell and taste they may begin to eat less.

Chapter 17
My Internal Organs

When I was a child and teenager, there was no such thing as having my blood pressure taken. I seldom even went to a doctor. The only blood pressure symptom I had was that sometimes when I stood up from a sitting or lying position, I would get dizzy and have to bend over for a few seconds. This, I have been told, is from low normal blood pressure.

I always knew that my heart pumped blood but now I am amazed at how hard my heart really works for me every day. Blood, with its important oxygen and nutrients, is pumped from my heart through my vessels to the distant cells of my body. When it returns through my veins the de-oxygenated blood is routed to my lungs to receive more oxygen. A blood cell that leaves my heart takes about twelve seconds to travel to my toes and back. My heart pumps the equivalent of about six litres (1.3 gallons) of blood every minute which adds up to about 9100 litres (2,000 gallons) of blood each day. This non-stop movement causes constant stretching and contracting of my blood vessels.

My vascular system is my body's weakest link. I was not thrilled to learn that one of the problems that might affect me as I enter elder age is the deterioration of my heart and blood vessels.

Blood pressure is the force of my blood pushing against the walls of my arteries every time my heart pumps and it is taken to measure the rigidity of my blood vessels. The pressure is at its highest when my heart beats. This measurement is called systolic and is the power at which my heart pumps blood through my arteries. It falls when my heart rests, known as diastolic, and shows the resting pressure in my arteries between heart beats. Blood pressure is at its lowest when I sleep and rises when I get up and move through my day.

My arteries need to be elastic and strong to do their work, for when the blood flows along them, it creates what is called shear force or drag, much like the water of a river sliding along its banks. If my arteries aren't pliable, this shear force scratches or erodes the lining of the artery. The result is that plaque accumulates, and blood clots can form.

Arteries, narrowed by plaque build-up, have a disease known as atherosclerosis. If the artery walls are thickened and they have lost their elasticity, that is a disease called arteriosclerosis or hardening of the arteries.

If I have either one of those my heart has to pump harder to force blood through my body. This extra force can damage the walls of my arteries and cause them to rupture. This is known as an aneurysm.

As the cells of my blood are forced through the arteries, the narrow uneven walls cause them to bounce erratically which can damage them. These bruised cells clump together to form clots.

High blood pressure increases the risk of stroke or aneurysm, plus there is the danger of heart and kidney failure. Anyone at any age can have high blood pressure. Once it develops it lasts for the rest of their life and the sad news is that nine out of ten people in their mid-fifties may already have or are developing high blood pressure. There are few, if any, signs of it so they won't know about it until they have a blood pressure test or until an organ suddenly fails.

High blood pressure is a disease, not a sign of older age, and it can be prevented.

As my heart ages there may be a decrease in: the number of muscle cells; the elasticity of my heart muscle and my blood vessels; the blood flow to my heart and some organs; and in the strength of my muscle. The valves, which open and close 100,000 times each day, could become stiffer, fatty deposits and calcium deposits may appear in the blood vessels, and there might be a greater resistance to blood flow. All this can result in an increase in my blood pressure and my heart rate, a decrease in the function of some of my organs, a shortness of breath, a loss of balance, and coldness.

Usually, by the time someone has developed heart damage or had a heart attack, they have been doing things wrong in their life for up to forty years. This information scared me because I had been eating wrong for about forty years before my research began.

I now ask my doctor what my blood pressure is each time it is taken. When I have had the time to relax for the required five minutes it is usually about 107/70. When it is taken just after I sit down or while I am talking with the doctor it goes up to around 120/80. Blood pressure is one of the important factors for longevity and as long as I can maintain it for the rest of my life my chances of reaching 120 years of age are excellent.

A year into my research I had to attend the funeral of Mike's older sister, Yvonne, who had died of a massive heart attack. Of Mike's three older siblings she came the closest to reaching the age of sixty. Her longevity was fifty-nine, not even half of our maximum life span.

* * *

Every day I breathe about 23,000 times which brings in over 11,000 litres of air, containing many gases, into my lungs. My lung's role is respiration, the process of oxygen transference. With each breath the air flows through my nose and mouth and down into the tube-like trachea. This tube, called a bronchus, branches into my two lungs. From there the bronchus subdivides into millions of smaller bronchioles, and these end in terminal bronchiole. On the end of the bronchiole are clusters of what looks like grapes called the alveoli. These are surrounded by capillaries.

Cells containing carbon dioxide, a waste gas from the metabolism of food, are transferred from the capillaries through the walls of the alveoli. My lungs clean the cells before they head back to my heart again. At the same time the new blood cells that are sent from my heart to my lungs are pushed through the walls and are picked up by the capillaries for distribution through my body.

My lungs do this process by the production of a chemically balanced fluid which makes the correct gas exchange.

I do not smoke, although there have been times in my life when I tried cigarettes. The first one was when I was about eight. A friend of mine came running over to show me two cigarette papers and some matches she had stolen from her father. I didn't know what to do with them, so she explained that we rolled something in them and smoked them, just like she had seen her father do. She thought that substance was grass. I had seen my father with cigarettes but hadn't suspected they were made of grass.

We hid in some tall, dry grass behind an old freezer in her backyard. We folded pieces of grass then she attempted to roll one of the papers around them. It was pretty flimsy and burst into flame when she tried to light it. She dropped it and we had to quickly stamp out the fire before it spread. We never did try the second one.

The next two times were high school. A friend and I were skipping class and hiding in the girl's bathroom when she offered me a cigarette. Wanting to act cool I took one and lit it. We were in separate stalls so she couldn't see that I didn't inhale. We were also on the same baseball team and when we were at a game we hid in some bushes and had a smoke. Again, I didn't inhale but took a mouthful of smoke and blew it out like she did. If she noticed she didn't say anything.

My last attempt was after I was married and had my first child. My husband smoked and I thought maybe I should too. I figured it would help curb my overeating. I bought a package of cigarettes when we went shopping and put them in the cupboard but since smoking wasn't a habit, I forgot about them for a couple of days. When I did remember I lit one, tried a couple of puffs and put it out. Again, it was a while before I thought about them and had another one. I was walking with it between my fingers when I turned around and saw my three year-old son following behind me holding an ash tray. I thought about how absurd the scene was and gave the package to my husband. I never tried again.

More than one billion smokers around the world are inhaling over 4000 chemicals with every breath. Many of those chemicals are known carcinogens and poisons: hydrogen cyanide–gas chamber poison; arsenic–rat poison; acetone–nail polish remover; benzene–gas additive; and ammonia are examples. Smoking also introduces carbon monoxide, which is a deadly toxin to their body.

Cigarette smoke destroys the cilia of their lungs. Ironically, the cilia are what is supposed to protect their lungs from toxins. Smoking, even secondhand smoke, leads to stiffer arteries, which is a known cause of heart disease. This increases resistance in their arteries and makes their heart work harder. Smoking raises their risk for bronchitis, lung disease, cancer, heart failure, and strokes. The Institute for Health Metrics and Evaluation states that nearly eight million deaths worldwide are related to tobacco and its uses, with as many as 500,000 of them occurring in North America.

Smoking also produces free radicals, and it is a toss-up whether fats in foods or cigarettes, with their nicotine and tar, are the worst promoters of free radicals. By inhaling just one puff of smoke, smokers are unleashing millions of free radicals in their lungs. Their white cells are then activated and that triggers an inflammatory response in all their organs. Tobacco smoke causes a constriction of blood vessels which reduces blood flow and raises blood pressure. As high as 80% of lung cancer is caused by smoking.

I have never inhaled cigarette smoke from a cigarette in my hand. Because of that I consider that I have never smoked. But I have always lived with smokers. My father smoked and my first husband smoked. Mike smoked most of our marriage.

His favourite time was when reading in bed. I would wake up to a hazy, stinky room and try to go back to sleep fast so as not to be conscious of the smell. Finally, I asked him to quit smoking in the bedroom. He was good about it and agreed. But the house on evenings and weekends was still rank. I tried to air it out by leaving the windows and doors open in the summer and opening the door for a short period during the day in the winter.

We had been married about twenty-four years when I learned that inhaling second-hand smoke is the same as if I smoked four cigarettes a day. I was really scared when I found out that an estimated 40,000 tobacco-related deaths in North America are from second-hand smoke. Second-hand smoke has about 250 toxic chemicals and inhaling may have increased the chances of me eventually developing heart disease, lung cancer, or respiratory problems, and could lead to me having a heart attack. And there is no risk-free level. Even short exposure can be damaging.

In every age group, smokers die at an earlier age than non-smokers. They also die at a greater rate from every disease. Non-smokers living with smokers have a lower life expectancy.

The day I learned all this is the day I finally said to Mike. "I can't do anything about you trying to kill yourself, but I do resent the fact that you could be killing me, too." He quit smoking in the house.

I hope, after about fifty years of breathing in second-hand smoke, that I was not too late in standing up for myself. After reading about how harmful secondhand smoke can be, when I went for my next check-up I asked for a chest x-ray explaining that I had lived with smokers for most of my life. I was pleased that it came back clear.

In September of 2008, after forty-eight years of smoking, Mike had his last cigarette. He was sixty-one years-of-age. He had a chest x-ray and then a CT scan. Amazingly, his lungs showed little damage.

If a smoker quits they can improve their circulation as the level of carbon monoxide in their system is lowered. Their pulse and blood pressure returns to normal and their sense of taste and smell increases. This is true because Mike used a lot of salt on his food when he smoked. Within a couple of days of him quitting he was complaining that there was too much salt in the food he was eating, and he had to cut back.

Those who quit will live longer than those who don't. After about ten years of non-smoking an ex-smoker has between a 30-50% less chance of dying from lung cancer than someone who continues smoking. And those who quit before they reach fifty years of age have half the risk of dying in the next sixteen years than those who don't. Quitting also reduces the perils of developing other cancers.

Smoking seems to have a great influence on appearance. It depletes skin of oxygen and nutrients and in smokers more wrinkles, more excess skin, poor skin quality, and more gray hair are noticeable.

Women fare far worse than men when it comes to the hazards of smoking. Nicotine is more addictive for them, and they have twice the risk of heart attacks, strokes, and lung cancer than male smokers. They also have an increased chance of developing other types of cancer.

During my early years, my lungs had a large reserve capacity. My lung function peaked somewhere between my late teens and early twenties and this might be due to me being more active during those years. After that it supposedly declines by about 1% each year for the rest of my life. In a smoker that decline doubles to 2% per year.

If my lungs are made to work hard throughout all my life, then I won't have to worry about those problems occurring. The good news is my lungs will never lose their ability to make the chemically balanced fluid for the gas exchange.

* * *

My kidneys are two bean shaped organs that lay near my spine at the small of my back. They are about 10 cm (4 in) long and about 6.4 cm (2.5 in) wide. Their main function is to remove waste products and toxins from my blood and send them out of my body in my urine. They conserve salts, electrolytes, and water.

Kidneys also secrete a hormone that stimulates the production of red blood cells. This hormone helps to sustain injured heart and brain cells and it plays a role in delivering oxygen to my cells.

My kidneys may begin to shrink in size and the vessels that bring the blood to my filtering system could start to stiffen and narrow as I grow older. Blood flow through this system may then be hampered so there is less blood available for cleansing. Thus, there could be more waste left in my blood stream. A blockage in my kidney can cause hypertension.

Kidney stones are formed when the urine is so concentrated that, first small crystals, and then stones are formed. The best way to prevent the problem is to drink lots of water which dilutes the urine and reduces the susceptibility towards crystal formation. Diabetes, though, is the most common cause of kidney failure.

Although I have two kidneys, I only need one to maintain life.

* * *

My liver has a multitude of functions including breaking down the fats I ingest, converting glucose to glycogen, maintaining a proper level of glucose in my blood, processing the harmful toxins from my blood, and storing vitamins and minerals. It makes bile, a yellow/greenish substance that aids in digestion. My liver also produces about 80% of the cholesterol in my body.

In some people as they age, certain enzymes produced by the liver are less efficient and the liver's ability to metabolize some substances, such as medications, lessens slightly. This can have a detrimental effect on the organ and could lead to a buildup of drugs in their system. Toxins, such as alcohol, cause more damage in an older liver, and cell repair is slower in some elder adults.

My liver's colour may change from light to dark brown and its size and blood flow may decrease. However, my liver function should remain relatively normal as I age.

I learned a good way to detoxify my liver is to drink lemon juice. Although it tastes acidic, lemon juice has an alkalizing effect once ingested. I occasionally add lemon juice to my morning glass of water. Lemon juice also will lessen my chances of developing kidney stones.

While my pancreas decreases in weight as I grow older, it does not lose function so that fat and carbohydrate absorption are not affected. However, insulin secretion may slow and insulin resistance (when tissues stop reacting as they should to insulin) may increase.

My bladder has two functions: expand to hold the accumulating urine sent from my kidneys, and empty out completely when voiding. Over time my bladder's ability to expand and contract may diminish, and I won't be able to store as much urine as I once could. Also, when I was in my twenties and thirties, the mechanism that told me to start looking for a bathroom sent a signal when my bladder was about half full. As I grow older that signal will come when my bladder is almost full.

I am taking care that I don't do anything that may harm any of these organs as I grow older. I need them in perfect working order if I wish to live to my full potential.

* * *

My digestive system consists of my mouth, esophagus, stomach, small intestine, pancreas, liver, large intestine, kidneys, and anus.

As I eat, saliva is excreted to mix with the foods, while my teeth grind them into a slurry. Saliva not only helps digest my food, it also allows my taste buds to have maximum encounter with the various flavours and it protects my mouth from bacterial infection.

The food is then swallowed and transported through my esophagus, by way of a reflexive series of muscles, to my stomach. A muscular ring or valve, called a sphincter, lets the slurry into my stomach then closes tightly to keep my stomach's caustic acids, or gastric juices, from escaping up to my throat and causing heartburn.

The gastric juices and other fluids are worked through the food in my stomach much like a washing machine washes clothes. This turns it into a smooth liquid, called chyme. The chyme enters my small intestine, which is between 6.7 and 8 metres (22 and 26ft) in length. My intestine has small fingers, named villi, along its sides and they absorb the nutrients from the chyme as it is sloshed back and forth.

My liver makes a yellowish bile that is stored in my gallbladder between meals. When I eat, it is squeezed from my gallbladder into my small intestine to help absorb the fats I have consumed. My pancreas adds a soda-like solution that neutralizes my stomach acids in the chyme and sends in chemicals to break down the proteins and sugars. These are sent to my blood. The remains of the meal are solidified by the removal of water and compacted into waste material for elimination.

My blood is now filled with new molecules extracted from the food. My kidneys filter the blood and remove the waste which is excreted as urine.

Indications of poor gut health are coughing, bloating, acid reflux, burning sensation, and indigestion. Like most people I do occasionally suffer from these, but it never develops into anything serious, so I feel my digestive tract is in good working order. But I have to admit that my eating is rather bland, no spices, no herbs, no pepper, little salt. It has nothing to do with my taste buds or with the spices upsetting my stomach. It has everything to do with the fact that the spices and pepper burn my tongue and mouth. Even when I ask for mild sauces or dips, they are usually too hot for me. It wasn't until I read about how hard spices can be on my stomach, and I know of so many people with stomach problems who like spicy foods, that I was glad for my sensitive mouth.

It has been estimated that as high as 40% of the population has some sort of digestive problem, which could lead to having to take drugs or even surgery. So far I am not in that percentage.

As a child I can remember being told to chew my food thirty-five times before swallowing. There was no explanation as to why, except that it was good for me. I did try it but didn't like the slimy mess that was produced. I have always liked to put a lot of food in my mouth when I eat. I guess it has to do with feeling the food with all parts of my mouth. And I didn't chew it very well, preferring to swallow it and fork in the next mouthful.

But, as with everything else to do with the food I ate, I learned better when I read about my digestive system. It's not surprising that I was treating it badly by not fully chewing my food and mixing it well with the saliva in my mouth. I now try to keep my food in my mouth longer. By doing this I am helping my whole gastro/intestinal process work better.

For most, aging has little effect on the function of their digestive system. In general, the progression of food down the esophagus is not impaired. Because of lesser elasticity, the stomach cannot hold as much food, and the food does not empty into the intestines as quickly, but these have few, to no, symptoms. There is limited impact on the secretion of stomach juices such as acid and pepsin, but atrophic gastritis, a condition that decreases stomach acid, may be more apparent in an elder adult.

My stomach is coated with a layer of mucus that protects it from the digestive fluids. When that is eroded away in some people by alcohol, spicy foods, or infection, they could develop a stomach ulcer.

Movement of food through, and absorption of nutrients from, my smaller intestine shouldn't change much as I age. Although the villi rejuvenate every 3-5 days, they do lose some of their ability to absorb certain molecules such as calcium. Lactose intolerance and too much growth of certain bacteria could lead to bloating, frequent heartburn, burping, passing gas, and discomfort after eating. This growth in bacteria may also lead to a decrease in nutrient absorption.

There are no functional problems with the large intestine as I age.

When I look at my years of eating the wrong foods, of not chewing properly, and letting it sit in my intestines due to occasional constipation, I am so thankful that no harm has been done to my digestive tract.

Chapter 18

My Hormones

Until I began this journey I really didn't know much about hormones except that they may have been one of the causes for the pimples I had when I was a teenager, they made teenage boys horny, and they were blamed for just about anything that went on in my body.

Since then, I have discovered that hormones are molecular messengers at the centre of my internal communication system. They regulate everyday processes in my body and their levels do change as I age. They are potent biological agents, often with complex and multiple side effects and are usually released in my body on a tight, co-ordinated schedule.

Most of my hormones are produced by my endocrine glands, which are the pineal, pituitary, thyroid, and adrenal. Others are made by my organs such as my heart, stomach, and small intestine, and by my ovaries. Some hormones control the level of other hormones, while additional ones work in pairs with one doing the opposite task of the other.

Hormones travel via my bloodstream to my tissues and organs and affect my growth, metabolism, reproduction and sexual function, and my mood. They regulate my water supply, my body heat, and my energy. They are tied to my brain and without optimal hormone levels, my brain won't function well.

There are hundreds of different hormones in my body. They peaked in my twenties and then stayed the same into my forties. As I continued to age they began to decline, as did the machinery in my cells and tissues for responding to the hormones. By age seventy I may have lost over 50% of the vital hormones I had in my twenties.

A few of the pre-conceived signs of aging in people are: their resting heart rate increases; they may suffer from more aches and pains; it takes longer for a sore to heal; they may lose or gain weight; there is a loss of muscle mass; they develop osteoporosis; there is an increased risk of heart attacks and strokes; and there is a decline in their immune system, causing them to get sick easily.

I guess I went through menopause in my early fifties. It is hard to know because I never really had many symptoms. I had two hot flashes in my late thirties. At least that is what I think they were. It seemed as if every pore in my body shot out sweat at the same time. Since it only happened twice I never said anything to my doctor. I had my last period two months after my father died and I have had no symptoms since.

Hormone replacement therapy, HRT, for women has been advocated for years. Estrogen was first given to menopausal women in the 1940s. In the 1960's and 1970s, *Premarin,* a form of estrogen, became popular. Estrogen replacement was hyped as being the best thing to prevent memory loss, depression, lower sex drive, and hot flashes. Then in the mid-1970s it was discovered that there was an increased risk of developing cancer of the uterus lining if taken for more than five years.

By adding progestin, which is a synthetic form of the hormone progesterone, to the estrogen the risk was reduced. Today there are about twenty million women on hormone replacement therapy.

Besides combating the side-effects of the "change" taking estrogen replacement is supposed to reduce bone loss and the danger of cardiovascular disease and it may delay the onset of diabetes in some women.

However, besides touting the benefits of the therapy, the Mayo Clinic also mentioned there was a downside. Taking the therapy may increase the chance of developing ovarian cancer by 20%. During the first year of treatment the possibility of deep-vein thrombosis doubles for some women. There is a heightened risk of heart attack, stroke, and blood clots during the first two years of use, and of acquiring breast cancer after four years of use.

HRT is also linked to small increases in womb cancers. There may be a greater risk of developing gallstones and it could double the possibility of gallbladder disease. There may also be a somewhat lesser danger of developing colorectal cancer after three years of use and of suffering from hip fractures.

I was told I should go on HRT. I had been listening to the news items about the many studies showing that HRT was okay but I had also read the reports warning it was not. I believe in erring on the side of caution and even if there is just one study that states something maybe harmful for me I will not even consider taking it. Also, I do not like to take medication of any kind.

I will rely on my body to know what it is doing.

Testosterone is found in men and, to a lesser extent, in women. It initiates protein synthesis and skeletal muscle growth and increases bone density and red blood cell mass. It also enhances metabolic rate and encourages the release of the growth hormone.

Human Growth Hormone (HGH) is an essential stimulant of normal growth in young people. Those who don't have the right amount age faster and more severely. HGH improves the immune system, burns fat, and builds muscle. It promotes cell division and tissue repair. Up to a 14% decrease in HGH every decade has been a natural part of aging.

With a decline in HGH body composition sometimes changes, with a lessening of muscle mass and an increase in fat. Organs could begin to shrink. Taking growth hormone replacement will increase muscle and bone mass, strengthen immune systems, increase energy and well-being, and decrease body fat.

Some Baby Boomers are choosing to take HGH and many of the doctors who prescribe it call it "age management treatment." The people who take the therapy delight in the fact that it makes them feel young now. Many of them are not worried about possible side effects such as joint pain, abnormal growth of bones, heart failure, cancer, diabetes, heart problems, and high blood pressure or any other problems that may arise in their elder years.

As people age, their bodies manufacture less growth hormone. However, exercise has been shown to stimulate the pituitary gland so it raises production of the hormone. This, in turn, will increase muscle and bone mass, strengthen their immune system, raise their energy level and feeling of well-being, and decrease body fat. So, a good exercise program, rather than replacement may be all people need. And there are only good side effects to exercise.

Health Canada only approves HGH use for certain conditions like growth failure and muscle wasting.

Dehydroepiandrosterone (DHEA) is a steroid hormone made by the adrenal gland in both sexes. It does play, an as yet, unknown role in the manufacture of other hormones such as testosterone and estrogen. Its production is at its highest when people are between twenty-five and thirty years-of-age and then falls as they grow older, particularly in women.

It is believed that DHEA could be a shield against the negative effects of high insulin levels in our blood and it may also boost our immune system.

Natural enhancement of DHEA has been reported with physical exercise, various stress-reduction programs, meditation, and caloric restriction. DHEA is significantly higher in ten-to sixteen-year old athletes compared to non-athletes, just as testosterone, growth hormone, and bone strength are also greater in athletes. In other words, exercise keeps hormone levels up.

Melatonin is made from serotonin and is secreted by the pineal gland in my brain. It governs my body's twenty-four hour clock by regulating my sleep/wake cycle. Since melatonin is made during the night its levels are elevated in my body, peaking around 3:00am. When daylight strikes my eyes, a message is sent to my brain to cease the production and release of the hormone.

My pineal gland began about the size of a kernel of corn and shrank as I grew older. So did my body's manufacture of melatonin. Bad lighting, electromagnetic fields generated by power lines, and many of the electronic devices I use in my everyday life lead to the depletion of melatonin in my body.

If I stay up later at night than normal, the bright lights can set back my melatonin production. Exposure to artificial light at night may decrease my manufacturing of melatonin.

I do need plenty of light during the day in order for my brain to turn the carbohydrates I eat into serotonin so it can be converted into melatonin at night. In the summer, with its longer hours of daylight, that is easy because I have more opportunities to be outside. In the winter, with reduced daylight, it is harder, but I do try to get outside every day.

For maximum production of melatonin, I sleep in a darkened room and wear a mask over my eyes. Increased melatonin during the night promotes better sleep and gives my body a chance to heal itself from the damage done to it during the day.

The thyroid hormone, which reacts quickly to a change in its balance, has many functions. It increases oxygen consumption and heat production, regulates my resting metabolic rate, controls my heart's rhythm and rate, directs my waste system, affects my neuromuscular system, maintains my glucose and cholesterol levels, and influences the hormone, cortisol.

Cortisol is secreted by my adrenal gland. It could become a problem to my body if a stressful situation turns into a permanent condition. Too much cortisol results in increased blood sugar and insulin, wasting of muscle, bone loss, decreased immunity, and much more. Just a note: these symptoms are all on the medical establishment's list as signs of aging.

Researchers advise that if people have to take hormone replacement therapy they should do so in the smallest doses and for the least amount of time. Hormones are powerful. Too much can be harmful. They must be balanced in relation to each other. Just one out of balance can throw all the others, and thus the user's whole body, out of harmony.

It is believed that boosting the level of hormones to the amount they were when people were younger might reverse some aspects of aging. But, as hormones decrease with age, so do the number of hormone cell receptors. So, taking extra hormones may damage the body by speeding up its inner workings and causing burnout.

After everything I have read about them, I would not take them, as some do, as a way to ward off aging, since I already know, and have accepted, that it is not possible.

Chapter 19
My Brain, Memory, and Dementia

I was always quite smart in school although I never really applied myself. Through my first three grades I had the top marks in my class. In junior high school and high school there were years where I didn't have to write the final exams for some classes because of my excellent marks in the quarter, half, and three-quarter year tests. This, of course, was before the semester system when we stayed in the same classes for the full school year.

During my chemotherapy treatment after breast cancer, I was told about a condition called Chemo Brain. Apparently, the confusion, lack of concentration, and forgetfulness that I sometimes suffered while on treatment could last up to thirteen years. This scared me because, while I didn't always use my brain to its full capability, I didn't want to lose any of its powers.

The year after my chemo and radiation treatments I enrolled in a residential aide/care giver course at a local college. I was fifty-three years-of-age, making me the second oldest student. My final mark was 97.2%, the highest in the class. I then took a week-long advanced residential aide course. I was the first one ever to score 100% in that course. My fears about lasting Chemo Brain were put to rest after that.

As I was testing my brain I was also reading about my brain and the changes that could occur as I age. I was born with 100 billion neurons, or active brain cells, and billions of other housekeeping cells. Each neuron has one axon and up to 100,000 dendrites. The dendrites are used to receive information from other neurons and the axons pass on that information. This works out to about 100 trillion constantly changing connections which keep me moving and thinking.

While my brain may shrink over my lifetime, certain parts of it won't experience a cell loss no matter how old I become. In spite of losing as many as 100,000 brain cells each day after the age of thirty-five and not having them replaced, my mental ability should not change unless I suffer from depression, lack of stimulation, or loneliness.

My brain weighs about 1.2 kg. (3 lbs) and floats in a liquid inside my skull. It is 60% fat. Each of the neurons, or brain cells, hold pieces of information, and to keep my body functioning properly that data must be transmitted to other neurons. If it cannot be transferred then my body cannot complete the tasks I wish it to.

Although it is only about 2% of my weight, my brain receives about 20% of the blood circulated by my heart and uses about 25% of my body's energy.

My brain is divided into three parts, the forebrain, the midbrain, and the hindbrain. Each section has its own assignments, but some chores may overlap into other areas. The forebrain, or cerebellum, is at the top of my brain and makes up 85% of its weight. This is where motor impulses occur, and it is responsible for balance and coordination.

Information about my motion and position are processed in the cerebellum. For any movement of my body to occur, my brain must know the speed of my body and where all my limbs are in relation. It also has to know where I am in the space around me. The right part of the forebrain rules the left side of my body while the left part of the forebrain rules my right side.

A portion of my midbrain's job is to route the incoming sensory impulses to their appropriate centres. It also controls my body temperature, heartbeat, and fluid balance. My hindbrain regulates my involuntary activities like breathing and vomiting, and monitors posture and muscle movement.

My brain and nervous system control my senses, body movements, coordination, and all the organs of my body. They give me my conscience, my emotions, and my mental abilities, and oversee my reaction to changes in my life. They are responsible for my personality, the language I speak, and my reasoning.

My genes, and the environment I am in, constantly modify and stimulate my brain throughout my whole life. Much of my brain's development was controlled by my genes while the fine tuning came about by the interaction of my brain with the world around me. Everything I do each day affects my mental growth and growing is something I have been doing in all stages of my life and I will continue to do right up until my death. It doesn't matter what my age, my brain will still be evolving and assimilating information.

At various times through my late twenties and thirties, I tried to continue my schooling. I attended one semester of university before my second marriage. My marks were good enough in the courses I took that I didn't have to pay back my full student loan.

I took a bookkeeping course and was consistently in the 90% range on tests. On the final exam I was the highest in the class. I tried the first year of the Certified General Accountant course and also had high marks but quit when I found out how many years of hard work it would be before I would get my certificate. I just wasn't into long-term studying.

My brain has neuronal pathways. These are clusters of billions of neurons that are from one part of my brain but have connections to another part of my brain. A disease, like Alzheimer's or Parkinson's that affects a neuronal pathway, can greatly impair its function.

Brain cells do not divide so they must live with their waste products, some of which are hard to get rid of. It is thought that this buildup of trash is what slows down the functions of the neurons and causes the processing of information in an elder brain to falter.

As people age their brain shrinks and there is a lessening in the number of brain and nerve cells. Slowly, over the years, a few may notice a decrease in balance, slower movements, slower reaction time, and an increase in the time it takes to understand ideas.

So, an older brain may just need a longer learning time.

The National Institute on Aging has studied people they call 'cognitive super agers'. These elder people in their eighties, nineties, and beyond have defied the notion that cognitive decline and aging go together. Their memory function is as good as those twenty to thirty years younger.

The long list of influences that can cause some people's brain to age include: an unhealthy diet; smoking; stress; hormone imbalances; cardiovascular disease, which decreases the amount of oxygen getting to the brain; nutrient and essential fatty acids deficiencies; both prescribed and street drugs; and free radicals. High blood pressure may affect some people by causing mini strokes in their brain that hamper its operation.

The good news, though, is that the brain has the ability to heal itself. It can reorganize so that other areas of the brain can take over lost functions.

I've used different parts of my brain at various times in my life. As a child, the more I used certain portions of my brain the more they developed. The neuron connections in those areas grew strong while the neuron connections in the parts I left unused didn't evolve as well.

What I didn't learn as a child, such as playing an instrument, will be more difficult to accomplish as I age because those neuron connections were not cultivated and therefore cannot process the information. But it is possible for me to grow those neuron connections by learning to play the piano or violin.

Throughout my whole life, my brain has needed upgrading. As it is challenged to learn and do more, its function will remain high even when I am in my eighties and nineties and beyond.

Lack of physical exercise can lead to neural dysfunction like depression. Antidepressant drugs re-establish low levels of catecholamine, a neurochemical in the brain, to normal amounts. So does exercise. Physical activity may also restore the suppleness of the arteries, which supply the brain with nutrient-filled blood. This, in turn, improves brain performance.

* * *

I have been making memories all my life. My memory is who I am. It holds everything that I have ever done in my life, from my childhood to my adult years, to my children's childhoods, to my writing, to my travels, to my grandchildren's childhoods. It also defines my future because without being able to remember what I have done in the past, I cannot make plans and think ahead. And, of course, without memory it's as if, in my mind, I have no history, as if I never was.

My memory is tied to my mind. If I lose any amount of function of my mind, I could lose some of my past life.

Memory, though, is a skill that needs to be practiced as I age. Where before it was an unconscious effort to recall something, in my elder years it might take more of a conscious attempt. Visiting with family or friends and talking about incidents in the past helps keep them in my memory. If there is something outside the realm of family I wish to remember, then I can refresh my memory by asking someone or reading books on the subject or going on the Internet. Forcing myself to remember will keep my memory pathways working.

Memory also depends on my senses. Listening to a favourite song or smelling perfume or apple pie cooking always brings back memories. So, I must maintain my senses as best I can; I must keep getting out and seeing friends and family; I must keep being active. All these will create new memories and keep old ones alive.

Elder people complain of a loss of memory. But how much is actual loss and how much is just small acts of forgetfulness that everyone suffers throughout their lives? When a younger person forgets or loses something, it is laughed off. When an older person forgets or loses something, it is magnified because of their age, and everyone wonders if dementia is setting in. This is because everyone has been programmed to believe that their memories are going to fail as they grow older.

Advancing age does not mean a decline in mental capacity. My IQ will remain constant all my life. As I grow older I may be slower on timed tests, but I won't lose my vocabulary or judgement. There are few cognitive functions that will really decrease with my age.

Age does not need to equate with dementia. Dementia is a disease like any other and can be treated if diagnosed early and in some cases can be prevented. The number of people with dementia is growing as the number of people living longer increases. At age sixty-five one in one hundred may have dementia. By the age of eighty-five, the figure is one in six. Those elder people who are isolated from family and friends have a higher chance of being confused, dull, and disoriented.

When I finished my residential care course, I got a job working in a long term care facility. I looked after men and women in a dementia ward. I listened to them talk about their childhood as if it were the present or watched them cuddle a doll like a child would.

One man was dealing with Alzheimer's disease. Sometimes he was lost in the disease. The sad times were when he knew where he was and why. One day, when I was getting him ready for bed he thanked me for looking after him. I told him that I enjoyed helping him. He then asked me if I could help him with his struggle. It broke my heart to tell him that I couldn't.

There are many things I can do that will help stave off dementia. One is challenging myself with Scrabble, crossword puzzles, and playing cards or other games. But I must find mental challenges that are fun. Not ones that make my mind strain; ones that train it. I like to read and do it a lot, and as a writer I am always thinking up new plot lines for my books. Also, activities such as chess, board games, and puzzle solving can help intensify my memory and could lessen my risk of developing Alzheimer's disease by about one third.

Physical exercise can enhance the intellect of my brain. Fit elder people tested higher in intelligence testing than did sedentary control subjects. Activity that moves their body keeps the blood flowing smoothly through their brain so that it can receive the nutrients it needs. It also leads to more mental activity. Their ability to master new, and remember old, information is elevated by the changes in their brain after exercising.

I know I need to continue discovering new activities for that will require me to attain new skills, thoughts, and ideas. Learning another language or taking a college course will open other parts of my brain. As I am acquiring the new skill, the corresponding part of my brain increases in size. Once I have mastered the talent and it has become an automatic movement, that part of my brain may shrink again. This shows that the brain is capable of rerouting information when necessary.

When my mind is not active, the dendrites, which are extensions that pass information from cell to cell, can atrophy, much like my muscles do when I don't move them. By exercising my brain, these dendrites remain limber and keep passing their messages. However, if I only repeat the same actions, my brain will only maintain the connections associated with that activity.

Each time I push my mind in a new way I will be strengthening and improving the links between my brain cells. The best part is that my brain can create new connections simply by me using it.

In order for this to happen for me, I have come up with a few strategies.

I must not do the same routine every day. I mustn't let my mind get complacent. I have to stay curious about life and the world. My brain grows when it is challenged. The more I know, the more my brain has to work. If I keep my mind stimulated it will help prevent memory loss.

I should always attempt new things, try working parts of my brain that I haven't used or seldom use, and choose something I want to learn or like doing. By continuing to keep my mind busy I will keep it eager, I will improve my memory, and I will protect my brain from future decline.

Looking forward to tomorrow and what it will bring is an obligation I have to myself, for it is another day in my life to be lived as I decide.

I should never think I am old because I will become old. If I think that I can do anything and if my body is in good condition, then I will be able to do the things I wish. Therefore, the way to stay sharp is to keep both my body and mind working.

If, as I age, I want my mind to remain alert, then it is up to me to look after my mind now. I need to take care of my brain through proper eating, sleep, and mental and physical exercise, the activities that will keep it alive as long as I am alive. My body without my mind is a frightening prospect.

Foods with too much fat and sugar may lead to hardening of the arteries to my brain. Eventually, this could result in a stroke or even many mini strokes, all of which will have a detrimental effect on my brain and my memory.

I know that good mental health is important for my aging. Staying mentally sharp requires optimum memory activity, the foundation for any quality longevity program.

There are so many instances of elder people who maintained their creativity or became creative in their later years. The following is a list of people, both famous and not so famous who are keeping or who kept mentally and physically occupied or challenged throughout their lives. They are my inspiration.

* Shigemi Hirata of Kyoto Japan is the oldest man in the world to receive a Bachelor of Arts degree. He was 96 years and 200 days old when he graduated in 2016.

*Nola Ochs of Fort Hays, Kansas, is the oldest woman in the world to earn a bachelor's degree. She graduated in 2007 with a degree in history at the age of ninety-five. In an interview she said she thought it would be nice to get a job on a cruise ship as a storyteller. She went on to become the oldest person to get her master's degree in 2010 at age 98 and became a graduate teaching assistant at 100. Nola died on December 9, 2016, at the age of 105. Part of her secret to living so long was that she didn't keep track of her age.

*Tony Bennett, the jazz and popular music legend, was born in 1926. He began his career after serving in the Second World War. His first album came out in 1951 and reached the #1 spot on the pop charts. He released several more albums with many more number one hits.

Then in 1964 the Beatles and the British Invasion hit, and he basically dropped from sight. After years of almost obscurity, he began a comeback in the late 1980s and had two gold records in 1992 and 1993.

Tony was inducted into the Big Band and Jazz Hall of Fame, has sold over fifty million albums worldwide, and published his autobiography. He also is a talented painter with a studio in New York. Unfortunately, Mr. Bennett was diagnosed with Alzheimer's in 2015.

*At the age of 102, Eric King-Turner moved from England to New Zealand with his eighty-seven year-old wife, Doris, in January of 2008. Doris was originally from New Zealand, and they had been married thirteen years. He said he didn't want to reach 105 and realize that he had failed to take the opportunity to move to the other side of the world. He knew he would miss his family and friends, but he was looking forward to a new and exciting life. He died there at the age of 104.

*In Chicago, 114-year-old Virginia Call registered to vote in an election held there on February 5, 2008. She had quit voting in the mid-1980s when she moved in with her grandson.

*Edith McNish of Courtenay B.C. Canada, celebrated her 100th birthday on June 2, 2007. Over her lifetime she worked as a teacher, salesperson for stumping and ditching powder (earning her the nickname "The Dynamite Lady"), and school trustee. She was involved in community life while her children were growing up and volunteered for many years. She still attended teacher's luncheons, exercised, played bridge and whist, and visited with family and friends up until her death on March 20, 2008.

*Ruth Frith of Queensland, Australia, was 104 years old when she passed away in 2014. At that time, she was the oldest active athlete and held the Masters Games records in javelin, triple jump, discus, weight throw and many more events. She also competed in the triple jump, long jump, and the 100 metre sprint. Finding competitors in her age group is hard so she tried to beat ones in their eighties.

*Nora Hardwick of Lincolnshire, England, posed nude in a calendar at the age of 102 to aid a local football team. She was

Miss November 2007, and was standing behind a pub bar wearing a necklace and a strategically placed scarf. She died at the age of 106 in 2012.

*Actor George Burns was born in 1896. He worked in vaudeville and movies with his wife Gracie Allen. They started in radio in 1932 and moved to television in 1950. Soon after they set up their own production company. Gracie died in 1964 and George continued to work and produce but not on the same scale. Then in 1975 he starred in the *Sunshine Boys* and his career was revived. He won a Best Supporting Oscar for his role. After that he was in a number of hit movies, including the *Oh, God!* series.

George also wrote ten books between 1955 and 1991. He died forty-nine days after his 100th birthday.

*Actress Betty White acted and stared in commercials in her nineties. She died on December 31, 2021, eighteen days before her 100th birthday.

*Queen Elizabeth II of England set a record of reigning over her country for seventy years. She died on September 8th, 2022, at the age of 96.

*Anna Mary Robertson *Moses* was born on September 7, 1860 and is known by her nickname *Grandma Moses. She* was an American folk artist who began painting in earnest at the age of 78. She is a wonderful example of someone who successfully began a career in the arts at elder age. She was 101 years-of-age when she died on December 13, 1961.

Part Four

Toxins, Pollution, and My Setbacks

Chapter 20
My First Major Setback

After my residential care aide training I found a job at a long term care facility. Working there was the first major setback in my decision to try for my maximum life span. Many of the people I looked after were confined to bed or wheelchairs, although a few did manage to get around on their own.

Seeing the residents brought back full force the reason, at age fifteen, I had made the vow to die by suicide at age sixty-five. The seniors there represented the people I never wanted to become, and they were living in the place where I never wanted to be when I grew older. Plus, working there raised a memory of a childhood visit to an "old folks' home" as it was called then. I have no recollection as to why I was there. Maybe it was to sing since I belonged to a church choir or maybe it was a family visit to a relative.

What is still vivid in my memory is the elderly residents sitting in wheelchairs lined up against the wall of the entrance hallway so that we had to walk by them. Some scrutinized us eagerly as we passed possibly hoping for a visitor; some just looked at us vacantly; some didn't even know we were there. I felt very uncomfortable in their presence and tried not to make eye contact, at the same time wanting to stare at them because they were so foreign to me.

Now, I was looking after people in that situation, and I actually saw their daily life, a daily life that I did not want for myself.

Two residents usually shared a double room unless the family could afford a single room. Even then it was small with only enough room for a dresser, a television, and a chair.

Each person I looked after was bathed once a week but every morning their face, underarms, and private area were washed. If they are incontinent they were kept in a disposable diaper, called an Attends, adult product, or brief. Most people spent their day in a wheelchair, but some had the freedom of getting around on their own, or with a walker or a cane. A few were bed ridden. In the dining room those who could feed themselves did so, and those who couldn't, waited for their turn to be spoon fed their meals.

Sometime during the morning or early afternoon they were taken to their room and their adult product changed, hopefully before they wet their clothes. In the afternoon they dozed in their chair or wherever they were sitting, their heads hanging to one side and their mouth open, drooling.

A lucky few had a visitor.

For lunch and supper, the ones who needed it were served pureed potatoes, meat, and vegetables. Others could have regular meals. After supper they were taken to their room where their face and private area was washed again, and they were put to bed.

If they had no regular bowel movement, a suppository was given every three days and on those days they were left in bed and their meals taken to them. If the suppository worked and they soiled themselves they had to wait until one of the staff had time to change and clean them.

Twice a week there was Bingo for those who were alert enough to go. Occasionally a one or two-person band would come and play in the evening. Some were able to go out in the van to shopping centres.

The sad part was they had worked hard all their lives and they now had nothing to show for it. Their life was confined to a bed in a shared room, a hallway, and a dining room in a building with a hundred other seniors. All that they'd possessed during their lifetime had been sold or given away.

I was so worried, while working there, that they might be my future; that I would be one of them in thirty or forty years instead of the healthy, alert, independent person I aspired to be.

It took a lot of rereading of the books on longevity and looking at the Internet sites before I decided to continue my venture.

Lucky for my peace of mind in the fall of 2004 Mike and I moved to Nanaimo, on Vancouver Island. I found a job working in home care. I was a personal care worker and would go to senior's houses to check blood sugar levels, give baths, take them for walks, and do some cleaning.

The people I visited were in their eighties and nineties and were still living in their own homes. When I saw them working in their yards, volunteering, reading, going for walks, taking trips, participating in sports, and trying something new, I knew that was the way I wanted my elder years to be. Working with them strengthened my will to look after myself. It gave me one more reason to keep making changes to my lifestyle so I could, indeed, reach 120 years-of-age.

Mike and I then moved to Port Alberni, B.C. and I began working with mentally and physically challenged men and women. Most of them could not verbalize at all; many had misshapen bodies; some suffered seizures; others were autistic; some never had or had lost the ability to feed themselves; many could not scratch an itch when they had one; most were in wheelchairs.

That was when it hit me how lucky I was to have been given this perfectly functioning body. It gave me a whole new respect for what my body has done for me since my birth and a new resolve to treat it better than I had in the past.

Chapter 21
Toxins and Pollution

My sister-in-law, Iris, was a hairdresser most of her adult life, going from working in a shop, to setting up a travelling hair business, to finally buying her own shop. She had put on some weight over the years and joined a dragon boat team in the hopes of getting more exercise and that it might help her asthma. The next year she belonged to two teams practicing four evenings a week after work. And she began losing the weight she wanted to. When I saw her and my brother, Roy, at Thanksgiving dinner she was so proud of her new figure that she danced around the room with her arms in the air and her hips swaying.

By early December Iris had lost more weight and her asthma seemed worse. She was so sick that she even closed her shop for a few days. I saw her at Christmas, but she was barely able to eat, then had to lie down afterwards.

On January 1st I phoned to wish them Happy New Year's but there was no answer, so I left a message. Roy called me on January

3rd and said that Iris had gone to emergency on January 1st to find out what was really wrong with her. After some tests she was told she had ovarian cancer and, as Roy put it. "The best case scenario is that she has ten months to live."

Iris had a CT scan, and the results were not encouraging. She had cancer in just about every organ of her body and her doctor told her that there was nothing that could be done except to make her as comfortable as possible. A few days later she was moved to palliative care. She died twenty-eight days after the initial diagnosis. She was fifty-three years old.

About a week after her memorial, I watched a news item that stated studies have shown that because of all the chemicals hairdressers use each day, they face a greater risk of developing ovarian and bladder cancer, and non-Hodgkin's lymphoma. I have since wondered if her cancer was caused by the toxins she encountered in her work.

Long before Iris' illness and death I had done a lot of reading on the toxins in our environment. There are so many it is frightening.

So, over the years I have made many changes in my life and one of them was that I have taken chemical disinfectants and cleaners out of my house, opting for natural or green ones instead. My body is designed to fight bacteria and viruses; it is not made for fighting chemicals. It is at a loss on how to deal with most of the chemicals it encounters so it tries to get rid of them by sending them to my liver to be detoxified or disassembled and eliminated. My body also tries to discard toxins through my lungs, my skin, and my urine. If that fails it shunts them into my fat or my blood stream or somewhere else in my body where they will accumulate and could become harmful to me.

Most cancer cells are initiated, that is, take the first step towards becoming cancerous, by a carcinogen, certain hormones, and free radicals. Some carcinogens are cigarette smoke, the aflatoxin in mouldy peanuts, nitrosamines in processed meats, chlorine-based prescription drugs, radiation, asbestos, solvents, and radon. If toxic chemicals, which are found in my everyday life, bind with the DNA molecules inside my cells, they may cause mutations that speed up the rate at which a cell divides. Since some cells only divide fifty times then die, this obviously will shorten my life.

My body's efficiency is determined by my cells and they are the ones that are attacked by the free radicals, which are factors that contribute to disease and aging. Pollutants contain free radicals that cause chromosomal damage and impair cellular function.

While my body produces antioxidants to neutralize the effects of free radicals, pollutants can wreck my antioxidant defenses. My immune system is weakened every time I ingest or inhale pollutants.

Toxin is defined as any poison formed by an animal or plant organism as a product of its metabolism, especially one of those produced by bacteria. So technically, a toxin is made by a living organism such as a wasp with its sting or salmonella producing food poisoning.

Poison is a drug or other substance, not of biological origin, that is very dangerous to life and health. The term is usually applied to a man-made chemical. Today, however, biological and man-made substances are generally lumped together under the word toxin.

I live in a toxic world, a lot more toxic than my parents or grandparents. There are about one hundred thousand different man-made chemicals in my environment today with hundreds more being added every year. Up to 25% of these can cause cancer and other diseases.

My generation has been the guinea pigs for the synthetic additives and dangerous substances that are in everything from food products to cosmetics to medicines. There are pesticides, fungicides, herbicides, preservatives, additives, flavour enhancers, and colourants to name just a few. While some have been tested for safety, not very many have been tested to see what happens when they are used together. The problem is that I probably eat, drink, and inhale combinations of products with those in them every day.

Toxins in my food inhibit the operation of my enzymes and as a result, my bodily systems could become less competent. Pesticides, fungicides, and herbicides are extremely reactive with my central nervous system, and they may also be carcinogenic.

Yet I am consuming more than 100 times the amount of pesticides, hormones, pollution, and toxins than past generations. Their residue is found on fresh and processed fruits and vegetables, in meats, and in other foods. Washing a vegetable or fruit does not remove all the toxins, plus there is what has entered the fruit or vegetable while it was growing. The most heavily sprayed fruits are strawberries and grapes.

The irony of is that the pests and fungi that these chemicals are supposed to kill are developing a resistance to them. We humans are not.

Also, there is food irradiation and genetically modified foods. Food irradiation is the same as giving one hundred thousand x-rays to our vegetables or fruits or meats. It is supposed to kill bacteria and thereby extend shelf life. However, it destroys vitamins and essential fatty acids that we need, and leaves residues of chemicals that can cause birth defects or cancer.

Genetic modification or genetic engineering is the introduction of genes from one plant into a totally different plant, or from plants to animals and insects and vice versa. It changes the host plant's DNA and introduces new traits or controls old traits, to improve it. An example are apples that don't turn brown when cut. Genetic modifying has replaced the former selective breeding and mutation breeding. Some researchers say it is fine while others predict that it is harmful. It could take years for the outcome from these experiments to be realized. By then many people could have suffered because of it.

Each country has different regulations but for many people the meat they buy in the form of beef and pork may have residues of hormones and antibiotics that the animals are given to speed up growth and ward off diseases. The fat of these animals also contains high concentrations of pesticides, fungicides, and herbicides that are sprayed on the grains they are fed. The accumulations of these poisons are higher in beef and pork than in poultry because it takes longer to grow a steer or pig for market. One good thing in Canada is that it is illegal to feed hormones to chickens or to give dairy cows growth hormones.

Then there are the food additives such as synthetic dyes, aging agents, mould inhibitors, de-germing agents, preservatives, and emulsifiers. They are chemicals added to foods that change their appearance, texture, and nutritional value. Two of the worst are sodium nitrate and sodium nitrite which can contribute to the production of cancer causing agents. These are mainly found in processed and cured meats, such as bacon, sausage, wieners, and ham.

Toxins like industrial solvents, arsenic, and radioactive elements get into the water supply. These cannot all be filtered or chlorinated out. And while they are in minuscule amounts we humans can get disease from as little as 100 parts of toxin per billion parts of water. Daily exposure to toxins has been linked to kidney and liver illnesses, and to cancer.

It doesn't take much poison to kill my cells and shorten my life.

Mercury can be found in just about all seafood. The smaller the seafood, the less toxic it is. However, the higher up the food chain a fish is the more mercury it is getting from the smaller fish it eats. Therefore, larger fish have higher incidents of the poison in their meat. Tuna, halibut, sea bass, and walleye are just a few fish to be aware of.

Studies have been done that show chemicals and additives in our food are harmful but there are still others that claim they aren't if taken in acceptable levels. This made me ask the question, how many separate acceptable levels of toxins can I eat in my food or breathe in a day before the combined level becomes unacceptable, before they start to shorten my life span?

Regrettably, research isn't advanced enough to pick up on all the different chemicals that can be found in our water and food and to decide how they react together. Our research is just good enough to make those chemicals.

There seems to be more public warnings over the condition of food and other products than ever before and it is getting to the point where I am afraid to eat out or to purchase much food from the stores. Fresh, canned, baked, and frozen foods can be tainted with botulism, e-coli, salmonella, listeria, and Hepatitis A. Every year foods are recalled due to contamination with these bacteria.

On most of these recalls the people most vulnerable to infections or diseases are the elderly, small children, and those with compromised immune systems. This is another reason for me to keep my immune system working well.

And now it has been determined that some people who have had food poisoning as a child have developed a severe illness in later years. One woman who suffered from e-coli poisoning at the age of eight, had her colon removed at twenty. Other serious problems that could result are high blood pressure, kidney disease or failure, and diabetes, all diseases that affect longevity.

* * *

Pollution in the way of carbon dioxide, chloroform, formaldehyde, lead, and benzene are in the materials used in the construction of buildings as well as in the paints, glues, polishes, floor finishes, and carpeting. And everyone in those buildings inhale these in the air they breathe. They are also in what people take into their homes by way of dry cleaned clothes, permanent pressed clothing, oven and bathroom cleaners, furniture, plastics, cosmetics, hair spray, nail polish, perfumes, antiperspirants, room fresheners, and bleach.

As solvents evaporate, people breathe them in, and they are transported right to their brains where they can do much damage to neurons and cells.

I wore cosmetics during high school, putting on foundation, eye liner, mascara, eye shadow every morning before going to school. Plus, I used a lot of hair spray and perfume. When I married and moved to the farm, I still applied my make-up and did my hair in the mornings. My husband didn't like it, but it was part of my routine. Then one day it dawned on me that the only ones who really saw me were the pigs and cows, and they didn't care what I looked like. So, I quit the whole make-up process but kept using hair spray.

I have seldom used cosmetics or perfumes since, occasionally purchasing them for a special evening out or if going away where I might need them. After that I would leave them in a drawer. By the next time I wanted to use them, they would be old, and I would have to buy more. Now, I just settle on a little eyeliner and lipstick. I don't bother with anything else.

For one year I dyed my hair blonde. I just wanted to see if blondes had more fun. In my case, there wasn't any difference. My friends still treated me the same as they always had, as did strangers. After my cancer treatments I decided it was time for a radical change. I had my hair cut short and streaked and I wore it spiked. It was so easy to look after, and I liked the look. Then I grew tired of always having to get it streaked so it looked good and I quit, letting it grow to shoulder length.

Over the years I have heard about the harm that the constant use of hair dyes can do to our body. One woman I know developed an allergy to her hair dye, but instead of stopping use all together she looked for another type that she wasn't allergic to.

I do dye my hair a couple of shades lighter than normal. Since it takes months for my natural colour to be very noticeable, I only use the product twice a year.

When I used to clean my shower and tub with soap scum cleanser, I would spray the cleaner and let it sit. Then I would strip down, step barefoot into the cleaner sitting on the bottom of the tub and scrub the tile and tub. After that I hosed down the tile and had a shower.

Most shower cleaners contain hydrochloric acid, which is corrosive to skin and eyes and could damage kidneys and liver, or hypochlorite bleach, which is not only caustic to eyes, skin, and respiratory system but also causes vomiting and pulmonary edema if inhaled. And since people apply these in a small space they are definitely coming in contact with them and inhaling them.

I remember the first time I bought a new shower curtain. I opened the package and hung it up. The smell was overpowering and lasted for days, even when I opened the window. I spent as little time as possible in the bathroom because my lungs would begin to hurt. The next shower curtain I bought I hung outside for a few days before putting it on the curtain rod. Now I have discovered that some chemicals, such as those found on shower curtains, may contribute to memory loss.

Household cleansers, hair sprays, cosmetics, perfumes, air fresheners, spray antiperspirants, detergent bubbles, and other products increase the noxious air inside houses and other buildings then end up in the outdoor atmosphere. Any spray, gel, foam, and aerosol bottle or can uses chemicals to launch the spray out of the container. As high as 90% of the contents of these bottles and cans are chemical propellants that contribute to pollution in the air we breathe.

I have used the household cleansers like every person who wants to keep their house as clean as possible for their family. Little did I know that I could have been injuring my family and myself from the chemicals in them. Makes me wonder what damage I did to myself by being confined in the bathroom with the fumes from the toilet, tub, and sink cleansers.

But it's a good thing I am not a fussy housekeeper, and I only cleaned my shower that way two or three times a year until I learned better. Now I use natural products.

By making homes and buildings more energy efficient, people are sealing themselves inside with all types of toxins. One way to fight the toxins is to have plenty of houseplants. They will reduce benzene and formaldehyde and remove particulate matter. Spider plants, plants with fuzzy leaves, mother-in-law tongue, English ivy, florist's mum, and peace lily are some of the better ones to keep in the house.

When I had children at home I had lots of houseplants. But I slowly got rid of them mainly because I would forget to water them. If I'd known the good they were doing us....

At one time perfumes were distilled from flower essences, but now they contain natural materials, as well as, up to forty different compounds and 5000 different fragrances. Phthalates, irritants which could interfere with our hormones, are found in many perfumes. They do accumulate in our bodies but since perfumes aren't considered to harm our body functions like drugs, they are not required to be tested for safety.

Anything that is scented, like tissues, cleaning products, hair gels, body lotions, and deodorants, is synthesized from petrochemicals. These emit volatile organic compounds that could have the same toxicity as wood preservatives, dry cleaning chemicals, and paint strippers. Problems caused by these chemicals can range from eye irritants to nausea to damage to kidneys, liver, and the central nervous system. They may also cause cancer. The main reason for their potential danger to humans is that their odours are confined to small spaces like homes or offices.

Toxins in soaps and toiletries can be absorbed directly through our skin into our bodies. Because I have lived in areas where the water is hard I've always had dry skin. I rubbed on scented body lotion after my showers for over thirty years, never once considering the ingredients. Since my learning process I now buy non-scented, natural lotions.

Occasionally, I have made my own soaps using glycerin as a base and adding scents and colours. One time, when I was buying my supply of glycerin, the sales lady said she made her soap from scratch because she didn't know what was in the glycerin.

"I thought working with the lye was dangerous," I said, remembering that I had read it was a skin irritant and could also do damage to my eyes and throat.

"It won't hurt you as long as you wear gloves and a mask," she answered.

So far, I haven't tried soap making from scratch.

* * *

During the Covid epidemic everyone was encouraged to use hand sanitizer which most did with enthusiasm. Bottles and wipes were in all the stores, and I used them to wipe down the cart handle every time I went shopping. If I went to three stores I sanitized my hands three times, not washing it off in between. Most hand sanitizers use alcohol to kill germs because it isn't harmful to our skin, so I didn't mind using them.

However, I trust good, old fashioned hand washing to fight the bacteria and viruses I come in contact with. An example of when hand washing was effective in my life was when I was scheduled to take a vacation to Mexico with family and friends to celebrate my son's fortieth birthday. A week before, one of the group homes I worked at needed someone desperately to cover some shifts because of staff being ill. I agreed to work two days.

The first day I was with a woman who was coming down with the flu. She was coughing, sneezing, and feeling sick to her stomach. We stayed far apart during the day, and I washed my hands repeatedly, especially after touching anything she had. I was fearful after leaving work the first day but showed up again the next day. This time there was a different staff member who had just gotten over the flu. Once more I washed my hands often.

The following week I was on my way to Mexico and feeling fine. I attribute this to the fact that I have always let my immune system protect my body.

Since Covid, television and social media advertising for chemical cleaning sprays has increased. We are bombarded with commercials telling us that we have to use chemicals sprays to keep bacteria and viruses off all surfaces in our homes for the protection of our children. Unfortunately, cleaning agents and disinfectants may create respiratory problems ranging from asthma, to temporary upper airway irritation to obstructive lung disease. And the use of such cleaners could weaken immune systems and disrupt hormones.

I was raised on the outskirts of the west end of Edmonton, Alberta. At the time the city was small, and all of its industry was on the east side. So, during my childhood I was never close to any real pollution.

Since then, I have lived mainly in the country or small towns, so my total contact with harmful outdoor toxins has been minimal my whole life. A bonus because toxins and pollutants are more prevalent in our cities. But I now live back on the north end of Edmonton and dealing with air pollution.

Pollution and smog from motor vehicles and airplane exhaust, and industrial smoke can elevate blood pressure and may lead to the hardening of arteries. This, in turn, causes diseases that are associated with arteriosclerosis like stroke and heart disease. Toxic air exposure from sitting in traffic may lead to lung infections, asthma, and memory loss. It may shorten life and triple the risk for heart attack.

When chemicals, a leading source of air pollution, are inside they are very toxic because we are constantly inhaling them. When they escape outside, they add to the outdoor pollution. It is thought that consumer products, which contain ethanol, butane, acetone, fluorocarbons, phenols, and xylene, emit as many, or more, toxins than our vehicles.

There are more pollutants and carbon dioxide in the air we breathe than there used to be. The fine particles from air pollution get the farthest into lungs and lodge in the tissue. These can affect the immune system and may cause inflammation that leads to blood coagulation and to respiratory and circulatory diseases.

We are slowly choking ourselves to death as shown by the fact that Health Canada estimates there are approximately 15,300 deaths each year in Canada that are linked to air pollution.

Chapter 22
My Second Major Setback

As I learned about today's health care system I had my second major setback. I am so afraid of needing it as I age. It is in appalling shape: crowded emergency rooms; stretchers with ill people on them in hallways because of lack of beds; surgeries put off for months; shortage of doctors and hospital staff. In the future this will only get worse as Baby Boomers reach an elder age and need care. It is estimated that now 1 in 3 people are over the age of sixty-five.

The Covid-19 epidemic put a real strain on the Canadian health system. Covid patients took over hospitals and it seemed that if a person didn't have the disease, they weren't important. Surgeries, even life-saving ones for cancer or for heart disease, were postponed. Other life-enhancing surgeries, like hip, cataract, or hernia, were set aside indefinitely.

But the ones who suffered the most during the early waves of Covid were the elderly. Their risk of becoming seriously ill increased with their age and any underlying medical conditions they might have had. And another twist was that many of them lived in seniors' homes where the disease spread quickly due to their close-quarters circumstances. On top of that family and friends were not allowed to visit for months. So not only were they at risk of getting sick and maybe dying, they had to go through it alone.

* * *

The U.S. Center for Disease Control and Prevention says the overuse of antibiotics has spawned a rise in antibiotic resistant microbes and is partially to blame for an increase in infectious diseases since the 1980s. Antibiotics weaken the immune system by taking away its job. It's the old "Use It or Lose It." adage again. So taking antibiotics could be killing us.

I think, for many people, being healthy takes too much work; being sick comes with much less effort. They would rather go to their doctor looking for a cure than do any prevention. They want a magic potion; one they can swallow and have instant health.

It is human nature to look for the easiest way. That is why so many turn to the medical establishment to make them feel better, or to lose weight, or to cure their diseases.

When my husband, Mike, found out that he had high cholesterol, he was discussing it with a friend whose cholesterol was also elevated. She asked him what he was doing about it and he said he was eating more oatmeal and pecans, both of which help reduce cholesterol.

She laughed and said. "I'll stick with my pills."

Modern medicine has made it so easy for people to neglect themselves. The medical community is geared towards curing an ailment instead of preventing it. They are always looking for disease not for health. There is a pill or liquid or injection for ailments and diseases, and a transplant or replacement for organs and joints. So, people taking care of themselves is not necessary anymore and many have willingly relinquished their obligation to look after themselves and their body for a pill or operation.

People between the ages of fifty-five and sixty-five years-of-age may be given as many as eight different prescriptions in a year. Some over age seventy can take eight different prescription medications and two over-the-counter medications daily. That many drugs can lead to medication problems and thousands of people are hospitalized every year because of not taking their medication right. Hundreds more end up in hospital due to dizziness, falling, loss of balance, and dementia brought on by drugs.

NSAIDS–Nonsteroidal anti-inflammatory drugs are available over the counter or by prescription and include ibuprofen, acetaminophen, and naproxen sodium and could contribute to liver and kidney disease as well as bleeding ulcers. One woman I know takes ibuprofen every night before going to bed. She claims that it relaxes her, and she sleeps better.

In the past, influenza, tuberculosis, accidents, and harsh conditions were the main causes of death. In the 21st century cancer (Canada Cancer Society) and heart disease (Statistics Canada) are the two leading causes of death in Canada.

One of the reasons I am afraid of the medical establishment is that, incredibly, another of the leading causes of death in Canada, is iatrogenic–the reported result of complications from medical treatment. The Guelph Today newspaper stated that every year 22,000 Canadian die from medical mistakes such as surgical and anesthesia errors, poor monitoring after a procedure, and injuries and trauma during birth.

I do not want to rely on doctors and the medical establishment as I grow older. I have decided that I need to be at the front line of my own health care. I feel the best way for me to avoid lying on a stretcher in a hospital hallway is to take care of myself. It is my responsibility to prevent difficulties now, not wait until they happen and then think maybe I should have made a change sooner.

Most people work hard to avoid anything that causes harm to the outside of their body, such as wearing seatbelts, walking carefully on ice, and trying to avoid accidents, but they have no qualms about doing things that are damaging the inside of their body.

As much as 85% of all illnesses are the result of an unhealthy lifestyle. Basic choices like lack of exercise, bad eating habits, smoking, the use of drugs and alcohol, and negative attitudes contribute to serious ailments. Once the body has been damaged by misuse, medical attempts may help prolong life but rarely do drugs and transplants return an individual to normal health.

Most of the diseases that people could develop as they age are preventable. For example, 90% of Type 2 diabetes is caused by being overweight and inactive. A small part is heredity. One in twenty people don't know they have the disease and one in ten people don't manage their disease once they have it.

Other chronic diseases such as heart disease, lung disease, and heart failure are also preventable and when someone develops one of them it is with them until it finally kills them. Again, the people at risk for any of these are the ones who are overweight, have a sedentary lifestyle, bad diet, and some family history. With Baby Boomers aging without exercise there will be more health problems created than the health care system can handle.

Like everyone else I have been led to believe that poor health will be part of my life as I age. The fact is; poor health does not come naturally. It is the result of a poor lifestyle. And it is so easy to avoid those elder age diseases.

I am doubly determined to look after myself since reading about the following procedures. I don't want to have to go through any of them.

Kidney failure is one of the effects of having diabetes. Many patients, while waiting for a transplant, go on dialysis machines. This apparatus cleans their blood by filtering out the toxins as the kidneys normally would. The patient is hooked to the large machine for up to seven hours a day and this is done three or more times a week.

If an artery is 80% or more blocked by plaque, a blood clot may get lodged in it and cause a heart attack. Bypass surgery circumvents the clogged artery by grafting a vein from a leg or an artery from the chest and rerouting the blood through it. It is one of the most invasive surgeries and has a 2-6% rate of death. The patient's heart is briefly stopped and the breastbone is cut lengthways then pried open. The blood is pumped by a machine so the surgery can take place. Even if the procedure is a success it does not remove the problem from other areas of the arteries.

Balloon angioplasty is where a catheter, a thin, flexible tube, is inserted into an artery. It is guided to the blockage where a balloon on the end of the catheter is inflated to compress the plaque and widen the artery. A stent, or rigid tube, is left in there to prevent further blockages. Angioplasty again misses plaque formation elsewhere. It also damages the once stable plaque as it is pressed against it. Cracks may form for more plaque to build up. Stents could induce a strong inflammatory response in the artery.

I don't understand why some people continue to risk having a heart attack, or developing diabetes and going on kidney dialysis, or losing the use of one side of their body through a stroke when small changes to their lifestyle could help prevent them. I don't want to go through a possible third of my life as an invalid. I am maximizing my health and well-being now so that my life will be worth living as I age.

I realize I should not fear aging for I can't change it; what I should fear is being unhealthy, because that is within my control.

I do not want my health to come from a pill or a machine. I go to my doctor once a year for an annual check up to confirm that I am in good health, not to get a prescription to make me healthy. I don't have time to be sick. I would rather spend my days going on a hike, or kayaking, or travelling, or heading out on some other adventure, than being stuck at home ill.

Another reason for me to maintain my health as I age is that, according to Statistics

Canada right now there are an estimated 1.7 million unpaid Canadians looking after 2.3 million seniors. And family members make up a large share of those care givers. If they were to be paid it would cost about $5 billion and bankrupt our health care system.

Due to many children living in different cities or even countries and families being smaller, one in three seniors may not have family or friends to look after them. They will have to rely on paid help, which will raise their health care costs tremendously.

Unfortunately, there is also a shrinking number of paid care givers to be hired mainly because the wages are low, there are few to no benefits, and there is little hope of advancement. So, it makes me wonder who will look after those seniors who cannot take care of themselves.

It takes work and time to be healthy, but I know that the best gift I can give myself is to look after my body. My health is my most precious possession. And it is my possession. I own it. It is up to me to take care of it.

Being hale and hearty is the key to good aging and when I am 100 or 110 and still enjoying my life, then the hard work I am doing now and continue to do so, will have been worth it.

If there were no diseases, accidents, and medical miscarriages, some researchers believe the human body would even live up to 150 years. Dr. Joel Fuhrman has written many books and made videos about healthy eating for a long life. He has stated he is doing his best to prove that belief.

Part Five
My Fountain of Aging

Chapter 23
My Weight

On the whole, people are born healthy but, with their lifestyle, they can make themselves sick as they age. They abuse their good health by the choices they make.

One of the keys to my longevity will be maintaining my weight. I know that I need a certain amount of body fat to cushion my internal organs and to protect me from the cold, plus I should have a reserve in case of illness. However, and this I don't have to worry about, less than 13% body fat is harmful and some essential body functions will suffer.

Luckily for me, in spite of my years of overeating, I do have my weight back down to what is normal for my height of 170cm (5 ft 7 in). Most of my adult life I had a set point in my body of around 61 kg (135 lbs). I weighed that in high school and while I reached as high as 68 kg (160 lbs) due to heavy overeating, and as low as 48.5 kg (120 lbs) from dieting, each time my weight has gravitated back to my set point. However, in the past ten years, that set point has risen to 63 kg (140 lbs).

And this is the weight at which I can move my body as fluidly as I want, the weight where I can ask my body to do something and it will obey me, the weight where I physically and mentally feel my best, and the weight where I feel good in my skin and my clothes.

Many people, when they see how much I can eat without gaining weight say I must have a high metabolism. That could be true.

Metabolism is the number of calories I need to eat in a twenty-four hour period in order to keep my body at a constant weight. I have a metabolic set point which is a trigger in my brain that signals when I am hungry or full.

There are two stages to my metabolism. The first is consuming food and delivering fuel, via insulin, to my cells. The second is getting the fuel into my mitochondria, which are the power plants of my cells. These mitochondria process the fuel to manufacture energy, which my body then uses to reproduce new cells and tissues, to regulate heat, and to take part in physical activity. Glucose-based fuel sources deliver the maximum and most efficient energy.

I have a resting metabolic rate, which is the number of food calories I would need each day if I was physically non-active, and a non-resting metabolic rate, which is the number of calories I would need to consume each day if I was active. If I do not expend as much energy when I age as I did when I was younger, my metabolism will slow.

This means that the more active I am, the higher my metabolism will be and the more calories I will have to eat in order to maintain my weight. Also, the more muscle I have the more fat calories they will burn and the higher my metabolism.

I found a simple way to raise my metabolism. In the process of digesting complex or plant based carbohydrates, my body consumes twenty-five calories per 100 calories of plant food eaten. This is dramatically more than the three calories it takes to digest 100 calories of fat. Therefore, the more fat I eat the lower my metabolism, while the more complex carbohydrates I eat, the more calories my body burns to digest them.

My body burns fat and carbohydrates for energy before it touches the protein which is stored in my muscles. Eating is something I learned I have to self-regulate. I need to control what, where, when, why, and how much I eat. But within reason because if I don't eat for sixteen hours my body begins to think it is starving and my metabolism will slow down. It is my body's way of trying to preserve every calorie it can.

There are so many changes that could take place to my metabolism as I age and there is the possibility for the metabolic processes to begin to fall apart. It might become harder to move glucose into my cells. I may burn more fat than glucose. My mitochondria may begin to wear out and their efficiency could slow as they produce free radicals.

Because they no longer are needed to transport glucose, my insulin agents might begin storing everything I eat as fat and my body fat will increase. Also, as I grow older insulin may fail to give proper signals for the synthesis of protein which I will need to build muscle. I could begin to lose muscle mass. Another aspect of insulin is that my bloodstream may become flooded with excess insulin which now shuns the glucose so that both could build up in my blood. This could cause a problem with my blood vessels, eyes, ears, and kidneys to name just a few organs.

I have changed many of my eating habits so that my metabolism will continue to work at its peak as I age.

A friend of mine was overweight, bordering on obese, all the years that I knew her. Plus, she never exercised, and she ate whatever she wanted. At age seventy-six she had a heart attack while attending a family reunion. The only thing that saved her was that her sister recognized the symptoms and made her chew on an Aspirin. Then she gave her a spray of her own Nitroglycerin.

At the hospital it was found that one artery had a 93% blockage, and two others were partially blocked. A stent was put in her one artery, and she was sent home. In less than a month, she was dead from another heart attack.

Statistics Canada reports that two-thirds of Canadians are overweight, with one in four being obese. Obesity is the second leading cause of preventable death after smoking.

What most of the authors of the books I read and the websites I looked at agreed upon was that being overweight at age forty could shorten a woman's life by three years and an obese woman will lose over seven years. An obese smoker could die 13.3 years earlier than her normal-weight, non-smoking friend.

Someone who is obese at twenty years-of-age would have a life expectancy of seven years less than if that person was at an ideal weight at twenty. By maintaining the weight someone is at when they are twenty throughout the rest of their life could significantly reduce their chances of getting degenerative diseases like heart disease and Type 2 diabetes.

Carrying too much fat is hazardous. It makes people old before their time mainly because their body can't move the way it should. Any type of activity causes them to become tired and they have trouble breathing.

Obesity also damages their organs. Their heart has to work harder to pump their blood through all the fat, their digestive system cannot function properly, and their joints suffer.

Because of the excess calories taken in, their pancreas has to send out too much insulin. As the years pass it becomes overloaded and cannot keep up with the demand. Their insulin supply gets seriously depleted. This leads to adult onset Type 2 diabetes. And this trend is being passed onto the younger generation with some of them developing the disease as early as ten years of age.

The human body can only take so much weight before it starts to break down. Sedentary people put on weight as they age. In the four decades between twenty-five and sixty-five, a woman's body fat may jump from 25% to 43% while men may go from 18% to 38%. Physical activity will help keep most of that weight off.

A major cause of death are medical conditions that can be traced to excess weight. Being overweight or obese can worsen every chronic affliction and disease.

I first met a woman when I was in my twenties and she was in her fifties. At the time she was on a diet wanting to lose a few pounds she had gained. I remember wondering why she was worried about her weight. It wasn't as if it mattered at her age.

Apparently, it matters at every age. That woman lived to be ninety-two.

All parents want more for their children than they had. My parents' generation, because they had done without during the depression, wanted better for their children. I remember always having ice skates and a bicycle and my parents bought the first television in our neighbourhood. My generation, in turn, wanted to give our children more and in some cases that meant driving them to school, giving them money for lunch at school, allowing vending machines in school, removing physical education classes from the curriculum, buying them good tasting junk food, and just not wanting them to have to work hard for anything.

My children's generation passed that on to their children. Computers and cell phones have become a total part of, and a total necessity, in their lives. As they grew up they had many different types of games to play on their computers and game toys. These kept many of them in the house and away from sports and physical activities with their friends. All that caring has had negative results. Descendants of those three generations are now paying for the display of love by their parents by developing high blood pressure, heart disease, and becoming overweight or obese.

Some children, aged ten to sixteen years, spend about six hours a day in front of the television or computer screens or on cell phones and 90% of Canadian children don't meet the guidelines for being active. According to the World Health Organization (WHO) there are more than 1.7 billion overweight people aged fifteen and up and over 400 million obese people in the world today. And there are more than twenty million overweight children worldwide.

For most of our history the average life expectancy of our species has remained the same or has increased slowly. In the last century it took a huge jump upwards. Although more people of my parents' generation lived well into their nineties and beyond, today's lifestyle of less activity and unhealthy eating habits is putting a new obstacle in the way of we, their children, being able to successfully continue increasing the longevity of our species. It is believed by many scientists that because of this new sedentary way of life we, the Baby Boomer generation, could be the first progeny in a century who will not live longer than our parents.

My generation accepted the addition of chemicals and additives to our foods. My children and grandchildren are so used to fast food outlets, frozen entrees, and junk food that most of them know of no other way to eat. Because of this the incidences of diabetes, heart disease, cancer and many other diseases have been increasing for decades. Given the chemicals, food additives, altered vegetables, and foods that have been filled with fats, sugars, and trans-fats to give them a longer shelf life that people are eating, and have been eating most of their lives, those scientists could be right.

In fact, they are right. In 2021, Canadian life expectancy was 81.6 years. That dropped to 81.2 years in 2022.

Does this mean that our species' longevity peaked with my parents' generation? Is obesity, lack of exercise, toxins, drug use, disease, and poor diet going to shorten our lives and those of our children and grandchildren? Will we be the first generations not to outlive our parents? I am trying to learn all I can so that it will not happen to me.

Chapter 24

My Exercise and the Benefits From It

I have always gone to my doctor once a year for a medical check-up and he orders blood and urine tests. Each year the tests have come back the same. My HDLs are high, my LDLs are low, my blood sugars are normal, cholesterol fine, blood pressure low normal. One year, when I was in my late forties, he looked at my findings, then at my past results and asked me if I ate meat. I said yes.

He looked down at the papers again as if he thought maybe they were wrong. "You must eat very well."

"Not really," I said and explained my high sugar and carbohydrate diet.

"Then I don't know why you are in such good health."

"Maybe it's because I exercise," I said.

He nodded.

Exercise is the main thing I have done all my life that is good for me. It has offset my bad eating habits, and it has kept my weight down, for without it I know I would weigh about 136 kg (300 lbs) and probably have hypertension or diabetes and maybe have suffered a stroke or heart attack by now.

I know that being active is totally necessary for me to have the health I want in all my stages in life, and it is especially necessary for my longevity. I believe that exercise is the single most critical influence on my health. People I know who exercise have a more positive attitude and a greater incentive to be healthy.

There are many diseases and infirmities that most people think are due to aging, but which really can be prevented or alleviated by being active or by doing exercise. I believe it is a cure-all for many diseases in both the older generations as well as the younger ones.

The statements I live by are: Exercise will right what is wrong with my body. Lack of exercise will cause those wrongs.

My body is built to be active. I have 650 muscles in my muscular system, which is responsible for my posture and provides the strength and force to move my body. My muscles hold my body together, protect it from injury, and produce body heat. Although my brain directs my coordination, it is my muscles that follow those orders. Without strong muscles, my body will not always be able to obey those commands.

Some people's muscle mass may begin shrinking in their thirties and forties, and they may lose up to half a pound of muscle a year. By the age of seventy their body could have lost 30% of its muscle and nerves, which can affect their strength. As their muscles shrivel, their metabolism drops, and they do not use up all the excess calories they eat, meaning there is an increase in their body fat.

But muscle loss is not because of aging; it is due to lack of use. Not exercising muscles causes them to weaken and they turn flabby. And a vicious circle begins because the more out of tone they are the less people use them until they need the aids associated with *old age* like canes, lifting chairs, and scooters. Exercise will fight both their wasting muscles and accumulating fat.

Statistics Canada points out that the people most at risk for disease or early death are those who are sedentary. As many as 60% of Canadians do not get enough exercise to benefit their health and up to 25% are totally inactive. Not only are they losing their strength and stamina, they are also losing their quality of life.

It is within everyone's control to do something about the disuse of their body and, hence, to age well. Any type of physical activity can increase longevity.

I like my body being able to do what I ask of it instead of me being limited to what my body movement will allow.

My motto: Keep my body moving and it will keep moving me. It is up to me to tell my body to get up and do something; my body will not do it on its own. Never have I been watching television and my body suddenly jumps off the couch and does a dance, or goes for a walk. It will sit like a blob until I give it orders.

My first choreographed exercise after I left high school was with Ed Allen on television. He was handsome, with chiselled features, dark hair, and a muscular body. Oh, how I looked forward to our sessions together. He would give advice on the benefits of exercise as he was taking me through a half hour of stretches and strength training. I worked out with him every day that I could.

When I couldn't find Ed Allen's program any more I tried various exercises on my own such as 10 BX and aerobics which I read about in a book. I bought an exercise record with a pamphlet showing the various moves on the floor as well as an aerobic workout. At first I was slow until I learned the routines then I would listen to the record and do the exercises. I did these three times a week for a few years.

When videos came out I bought a couple to do step aerobics. I did them for years and then switched to walking/jogging a couple of times a week.

Aerobic (oxygen using) exercise could be in the form of walking briskly, swimming, bicycling, running, jogging, or dancing. It should be rhythmic and sustained for at least thirty minutes.

The benefits of aerobic exercise are a strengthening of my lungs, my heart (cardio) and blood vessels (vascular), and a lowering of my blood pressure. I like to walk/jog or bicycle about three or four times a week and my low to normal blood pressure is proof that it works.

As little as thirty minutes of walking briskly each day can reverse half of all the diseases and dysfunctions of most people. It will also save money on surgeries and drugs.

It has also been shown that there is a benefit to interval training which is alternating intense activity with lighter activity. That is, if I walk for exercise, then I should increase my pace for a minute or two or even jog for a couple of minutes then go back to walking. Doing interval training is supposed to burn more calories and improve aerobic capacity. It also makes exercising easier for people in that they don't get bored, and they don't need special equipment. Some trainers say that doing interval training for just fourteen minutes a day will get a person in shape.

I also like to take a brisk walk in evening whenever I can. It gets my metabolism working to use up the calories I've eaten during the day and contrary to what research states, I do sleep better at night after a good walk.

In one town we lived I was called a 'streetwalker' by our friends and neighbours because just about every evening during the summer they would see me walking past their houses, or along the lakeshore, or in the downtown area.

I also do two days of weight training a week. This is an anaerobic type of exercise, meaning it is aimed at increasing muscle strength and endurance and doesn't use as much oxygen. It is necessary to develop my muscles so my body can do the work I ask of it. Women who weight bear or strength train three times a week can increase their bone mass by over 5% and reduce their risk of hip fracture by more than 40%. Those who don't exercise can lose over 1% of their bone mass every year.

Flexibility decreases with age and muscles become stiff and joints degenerate. Stretching exercises improve the range of motion of joints and reduces muscle tightness. It allows muscles, joints, and tendons to remain supple and limber. This alleviates the impaired mobility so common in the elderly.

Without proper exercise, the muscles, ligaments, and tendons of the body contract. People begin to lose height, strength, and flexibility in their middle age. They also lose the free range of motion that used to come so naturally to them, so that normal daily activities become difficult and in some cases almost impossible.

I have always done my stretching exercises with my weightlifting and I added Tai Chi twice a week.

Gardening is a beneficial exercise, and it is also a relaxing past time. Not only are people outside in the fresh air, they are moving about and are smelling the wonderful, natural scents of the flowers and plants, a kind of aroma therapy.

I exercise in the morning and at home. At home, because I don't have to go to the gym, change into my outfit, exercise, then change back into my clothes and go home or to work. And in the morning to get it out of the way for the day. Then if I am tired or go somewhere or have company in the evening, I am not going to use that as an excuse to skip my routine.

Heart disease is the leading cause of death in North America for both men and women. Inactivity is a major contributor to heart disease.

Gaining fat, losing muscle mass, and being overweight by age sixty-five could mean a loss of 33% of the heart's ability to pump blood and 35% of the lung's ability to pull in oxygen. If people don't exercise, their heart muscle weakens, and the heart becomes smaller. Arteries will lose their elasticity and become partially blocked.

Regular exercise makes the heart stronger and more resistant to disease. Every time my heart beats, blood cells are being sent to the tissues in the rest of my body with much needed oxygen and nutrients. The stronger my heart, the more efficient it is in its delivery and the fewer heartbeats it takes to do so. This means my heart does not have to work so hard and therefore can perform its task over a longer life span. And it has been proven that a person doesn't have to exercise very long each day to begin scoring some improvement. And that improvement begins to show in just a few weeks.

The dangers of being unfit are compared to the dangers of smoking two packs of cigarettes a day. Even a person who is overweight, but exercises, is healthier than a slender person who doesn't.

If I don't use my body and keep it active, then it will slowly decay, and I will be miserable for a great many of my elder years.

I am responsible for my actions, even for my aging.

I have a friend who is in his mid-eighties. He spent his early years building a hotel empire but even though he was busy with his work and family, he still found time to play tennis, squash, and golf each week. He buys and renovates properties and still plays tennis, squash, and golf. We were talking one day, and I commented about how physically and mentally active he still is. His answer: "I'm not letting the old man in."

* * *

Once I reached adulthood, there were two reasons why I exercised. One was because it made me feel good, but the most important one was that I knew I needed it to compensate for my overeating and to keep my weight down. I knew that the more calories I burned the more I could eat.

But I found out that I have been reaping many more benefits than just weight control.

The explanation why, since childhood, that I have been able to eat what I want and as much as I want without gaining weight is because muscle burns more calories than fat does. Body muscle is active and expends calories twenty-four hours-a-day even when I am sleeping. In order to function, 0.45 kg (1 lb) of muscle burns up to 150 calories.

Conversely, my fat is inactive and 0.45 kg (1 lb) of fat consumes only three calories a day in performing its task of doing nothing. When I am not exercising, my body is still using calories and it is all thanks to the fact that I have muscle. And my body uses stored fat to feed those muscles.

Exercise keeps my insulin levels low even when I don't eat right. It also elevates my body's ability to identify and use insulin. This means my pancreas doesn't over-produce insulin in response to a rise in my blood sugar. It also allows my cells to use high levels of blood sugar for energy.

By making my joints move I can help prevent arthritis. My joint cartilage receives new nutrients every day as the old fluid is pushed out and new fluid enters to be soaked up. Without the nutrients, some areas of the cartilage may wear out and expose the underlying bone.

Movement strengthens my tendons and ligaments, and keeps my spine nourished by drawing in and flushing out fluids. Without exercise my spinal disks, which are the shock absorbers between the vertebrates, will gradually shrink and lose elasticity. The result will be that my body could lose height and my disks become more prone to "crush fractures".

My moderate exercising improves my mood which in turn strengthens my immunity. It boosts the function of the killer cells of my immune system and that is why I do not pick up infections and why I am seldom sick.

With exercise my body has better blood clotting, better organ functions, improved body posture and flexibility. It heightens my mental alertness and allows me to bounce back from injuries quicker. I have no trouble with my right ankle that I have sprained so often or with my back.

Exercise has kept my blood pressure low normal. It has lowered my resting heart rate to sixty-two and has increased my endurance.

Exercise makes me expand my lungs so that their tissues don't lose elasticity and become stiff. I don't have shortness of breath.

Another advantage I had from exercise is that I went through menopause without any problems: no hot flashes, no headaches, no depression, no memory loss. I never had to take any drugs or hormones.

I rarely have any trouble sleeping and I attribute that to my physical activity.

Bone density increases tremendously from exercise. With my strong bones, a fall will not be as dangerous as it would be if my bones are more fragile. Maybe that is why I have never broken a bone.

At eighty-seven, my mother fell down twelve stairs in church. Two doctors and a nurse were in the congregation and they made her lie still until an ambulance arrived. On the way to the hospital the paramedics cut off her pants to remove them, rather than roll her. After an examination, x-rays, and cat scans, it was discovered that she had massive bruising but no broken bones. I believe that the reason she didn't break a hip or some other bone, like many people younger than her do, is because of the exercise she has done over the years. She used to walk three blocks to and from work. When she retired she went for walks in the evening with my father, took up clogging and line dancing, and, after moving into an apartment building, at age seventy-eight, climbed up and down two flights of stairs.

As part of my exercise routine, I stand on one foot for a period of time which has increased my sense of balance. Weak muscles, along with poor balance, are believed to be a major cause of falls in older people. As many as 25% of women who fall and fracture a hip will die within a year. Many more will be disabled and confined to a wheelchair or a bed in a nursing home, the place where I most fear ending up.

Exercise keeps my good HDLs high in my blood.

Walking fifteen or more minutes a day for a total of ninety minutes a week can help me reduce the risk of developing Alzheimer's disease.

Exercise helps increase circulation of my blood especially to my brain. It improves my mental agility by keeping the arteries to my brain open, so the blood moves easier. It stimulates my brain's release of endorphins, which are molecules of natural narcotics. They give me an actual, natural high. I feel calm and relaxed after exercising.

My sister says she remembers once asking me if I ever got depressed and I answered. "No, never." And that is true, I don't. And I think part of that has to do with the fact that I know myself and accept myself so well, and part is because I exercise.

As I age, my body will decrease its production of the growth hormone. Studies have shown that exercise induces our body to continue its manufacture and release of the hormone which leads to the development of new cells in our brain. This is excellent news because it means that it won't be necessary for me to ever go on replacement therapy and risk developing cancer or heart problems.

As I get into my elder years my metabolism will probably not handle fatty acids as well as it used to. This could lead to a depressed immune system and atherosclerosis or hardening of my arteries. But the good news is that it has been shown that while exercising, my body converts free fatty acids into energy for up to 80% of the calories it uses to complete that activity.

Some evidence points to the fact that starting to exercise at a young age helps decrease the life-long risk of developing diseases including high blood pressure and diabetes. Lucky for me that I played outside with my friends when I was young, was active in sports in school, and have done some sort of exercise all my life.

Although, it didn't work for me, studies have shown that women who exercise regularly are less likely to develop breast cancer. Men and women who exercise could reduce their chances of getting colon cancer by 60%.

Years ago, when cancer was discovered in a woman's breast, usually the breast was removed as were all the lymph nodes under her arm. This led to her arm constantly being swollen due to the lack of nodes necessary to remove the fluid that would build up in her arm. When I worked in long term care I looked after a woman who had had such a radical mastectomy. Her right arm was so swollen that she couldn't move it. And she was in constant pain all day long.

Times changed so that when I had breast cancer the doctor only performed a lumpectomy. However, she also removed twenty-two of the approximate forty-five lymph nodes from my armpit to check if the cancer had spread to my lymphatic system. It hadn't.

I have since learned that my lymphatic system has many functions including collecting garbage from my body, cleansing my tissues, and carrying needed nutrients to my cells. It seems I have three times more lymphatic fluid than I have blood but unlike the blood that has my heart to pump it through my body, the lymphatic system relies on the movement of my body to keep it working. So, my exercising has kept the fluids flowing and my lymph nodes in peak condition as shown by the fact that I have never had trouble with my arm swelling.

Exercise or an increase in activity can begin to benefit anyone at any age. I knew a man who had a stressful desk job, who smoked and who had put on weight. When he got a job stocking shelves at a local store he began to lose weight. After a few months he went to see a doctor who checked his prostate, bowel, heart, lungs, blood pressure, pulse, blood, everything. When the results came back he was told that he had no prostate problems, his bowels were fine, he had a strong heart and pulse, his lungs were good, his blood pressure was on the low side, and his good HDL's were high and his lousy LDL's low. His weight was within range for his height.

The man was a bit surprised and said to his doctor. "But I smoke, and I don't eat very well. I like my meat, potatoes and gravy. I don't eat fruit or vegetables and I drink beer on weekends."

The doctor told him. "Well, apparently you are eating what your body needs. At the rate you are going you will live into your eighties."

One of the differences in his life was that he had changed jobs, going from a sedentary desk job to a more active one. He was using up more calories, plus the muscles he had developed from lifting boxes burned energy so he lost the excess weight he was carrying. When he was telling me about his results he told me to touch his chest. I did and it was hard.

"I've never had muscle there before," he said, proudly.

* * *

Fayja Singh, a British Sikh of Punjabi Indian descent, took up running in 1995 at the age of eighty-four. He competed in the 2003 Toronto Waterfront Marathon setting the record for ninety-plus years of age. He was ninety-two and ran it in five hours, forty minutes. When he was one hundred, Singh set eight world age group records in one day, running the 100, 200, 400, and 800 metre dashes, the 1500 metres, the mile, and the 3000 and 5000 metres. Three days later he became the first one hundred years old to complete a marathon, finishing the Toronto Waterfront Marathon in 8:11:06.

One of my greatest fears has been that at some point in my life I would not be able to exercise, because I know full well that the reason I am healthy in my seventies is because I always have been active. I know how lethargic and heavy my body feels when I don't get to go through my routines for just a week or two. So, I was afraid that if, for some reason, I couldn't do any type of activity for a month or more I'd lose my muscle mass, I'd gain fat, I'd lose my ability, I'd lose my agility, and I'd lose my health, all of which are the signs of the disuse of older age.

I also didn't want to lose my independence, my dignity, my self-respect. I wanted to live my life the way I had always lived it and my belief is that exercise will be the largest contributor to making that happen.

But then I began to worry. Would I still be able to exercise when I reach ninety or one hundred years-of-age?? If I couldn't, then how bad would my life become? How low would my health sink? How many of my 120 years would it cost me?

Then I watched a heartening newscast about a woman in Leduc, Alberta, who was still doing aquacise exercises at 100 years-of-age. Others in the class with her were aged seventy-five, eighty-four, and ninety-two.

What a relief it was to know that I may have to change the type of exercise I do, or the duration, or the intensity but I won't have to stop.

Many gerontologists believe that exercise is the closest thing there is to an anti-aging pill. I prefer to think of it as a healthy aging or an aging-well pill. It can make us feel better, look better, and live longer. The evidence is hard to ignore.

One year my doctor was on holidays when I went for the results for my annual check-up. The doctor who was replacing him said my glucose fasting, my sodium and potassium, my calcium, my alkaline, my blood and urine, and my HDLs and LDLs were all normal. I don't have any inflammation, which is the body's natural reaction to an injury or infection.

"This is unusual," he said. "How old are you?"

"Sixty-seven," I answered.

"Usually, people have some sort of illness by that age, but you don't."

How awful that the medical establishment *expects* people to have some kind of disease or sickness as they grow older and are surprised when someone is actually healthy.

It is sad that I am the exception not the rule, but I guess it proves that my exercising is working.

The World Masters Games were first held in Toronto, Ontario, in 1985 to promote and encourage mature athletes to participate in sports on a regular basis. The games want to prove that people of all ages can take part in a competitive sport, and that they can continue to do so throughout their lives. While the youngest is thirty-five, there is no upper age limit and no qualifying. Each entrant pays for his or her way, their meals and accommodation, and a registration fee. Each is competing for himself or herself, not for a country. It is all about personal achievement.

The word "Masters" does not mean a skill level; it is an age designation. With between 25,000 and 30,000 athletes from about 100 countries, the Games are thought to have the largest participation of any multi-sport competition in the world. Everyone competes with others in their own age category.

The games take place in different countries every four years. In 2017, the last before Covid, men and women in their seventies, eighties, nineties, and older competed. One man who was 101 years of age competed in the javelin throw, the shot put, and the 200 metre race. Two women (85 and 88) competed in the 100 metre race; one 81 year old woman ran the 5000 metre race;

and one woman in the discus throw was 90 years old.

In 2013 they were held in Turin, Italy. The oldest woman was in her late eighties and the oldest man was ninety-nine.

Two women competed in the seventy to seventy-four year age group, 8000 metre (8748 yard) cross-country run, while three men took part in the over eighty- 8000 metre cross country run. One woman was entered in the seventy-five to seventy-nine age group for the 8000 metre cross-country run. She finished it in just over one hour. Two women took part in the 5000 metre race walk in the 85 to 89 year old category.

Six men ran in the 100 metre dash in 90-94 year age group and three in the 95-99. One man entered the fifteen hundred meter dash in the 90-94 year age group and one man entered in the over 95 year age group. Seven men took part in the short hurdles 80-84 year age group and two on the 85-90 age group.

Three women ran in the 100 metre dash in the 85-89 age group and one in the 90-94 year age group. Three women took part in the 400 metre dash in the 85-89 year age group. Two women ran the 8000 metres in the 80-84 age group

And the list goes on and on. People in their sixties, seventies, eighties, and nineties and even over 100 years-of-age taking part in the World Masters Games, showing the world that enjoyable, active life does not end at any age.

Chapter 25
Planning My Elder Years and Erasing
the Prejudices Against Elder People

I do not recall ever having a conversation with anyone about their thoughts on their elder years. Most of us plan our education, our careers, our children, and then once that part of our life is in order we spend the rest of our time organizing for retirement. This, we view as a time of freedom to do many of the things we didn't have the time or money for when we were working and raising a family.

Unfortunately, the only plan many of us have for our elder years is to hope that we will age slowly and gracefully with our mind and body intact. Retirement and aging are not synonymous. Most of us want to retire in our early sixties. In today's world that is not old. Actually, if we look at 120 years-of-age as being our maximum life span, then sixty is only halfway.

I have made some long range strategies on how I am going to live my elder years. I still will continue my hoping, but I have also taken action to make sure I can enjoy them for I know they will not take care of themselves.

One of the foundations of my plan is that I must never think I am too old for anything. I must think of everything as a new experience in a life full of experiences. By continuing to grow intellectually and keeping my mind and body active, I will age well mentally and physically.

Some researchers say people don't live long enough to die of old age. So that means they die from something else, like an elder age-related disease, most of which are mainly preventable. I feel I am staving off those diseases with my exercises and by having changed my eating habits.

Where I am going to live is also critical. When I was a child I was told that I was independent. It didn't bother me because I didn't understand what it meant. But since then, I've learned more about myself. I don't like having someone do something for me. More importantly, why should I get someone to do something for me that I can do for myself? I am not an invalid.

Even when my back was sore, or my ankle swollen I would hobble around and get things for myself. I hated the idea that there was a chance that I couldn't. Because of this I have never wanted to lose my independence as I grow older, so I plan on living in my own home for as long as possible.

My parents had lived in their home for forty-one years when my father died. Mom continued to reside there but after three years found the yard work and maintenance hard to keep up with. She found an apartment to rent on the seventeenth floor of an apartment building and sold her house. She lived there until she moved into a lodge at eight-nine years of age. She died at the age of ninety-two.

I knew a woman who, at the age of ninety-five, was still living in her own home. Then one day while she was heating soup for her lunch she accidentally caught the sleeve of her sweater on fire. She didn't burn herself badly, but it did scare her children and grandchildren, so they put her in a long term care facility. When I visited, she told me how much she hated living there, that she wanted to go home. She slowly deteriorated until she finally died in less than a year.

I have wondered since how I would react in that situation. I do want to live on my own for as long as possible but since I also want to live to be 120 years-of-age, I have decided that when the time comes, I will move into a senior's home or senior's apartment building where I can still have my own place but also know that there is someone around if I need them. I kind of like the idea that someone will be cooking my meals and cleaning my place, something I have been doing for decades. What I do want to avoid is being in the situation where I have to move to a long term care facility and live in a bed.

Money is going to be important. I will only have a small pension from work so I will have to rely on my Canada Pension and my Old Age Pension. Also, I can write until I can't turn on my computer anymore. P.D. James, the well-known British mystery writer, was still publishing books in her eighties. Barbara Taylor Bradford's latest book was published in 2021 when she was eighty-seven.

And there is nothing to stop me from getting a part time job. It is predicted that when all the Baby Boomers retire there will be a shortage of workers. Even now many retirees are returning to the workforce for extra money or because they have time on their hands.

However, I am not one to spend much money. I've always believed that it is not how much money I make but how much I spend that will determine how much money I have. And since I will be in my own home for most of my elder years my expenses will be low.

What am I going to do with my time? First of all, I feel the worst thing I can do is sit on the couch all day in front of the television. Watching pretend people live pretend lives is a waste of my valuable life at any age. I have many important things I want to do in my life yet, such as: have a large flower garden; travel; write a great novel.

When I was in my thirties I dabbled in painting. I would like to try it again.

Then there is community work. I can get out and volunteer, visit shut-ins, help in the community, walk a dog for the SPCA, join a book club, or play cards. Having something to do gives me a sense of motivation and it has been shown that death rates decrease among people who have a strong purpose in life.

I have always stayed in contact with family and friends, and I will keep all my friendships alive. Rather than wait to go to a person's funeral, I will visit that person while he or she is alive. Or failing that, I can phone them and have a long chat, or do a video chat, or even write an old fashioned letter. One great feature of today's technology is e-mail. It is simple to use and an easy way to keep in touch. So is texting.

I studied the French language for eight years in school, German for three, and Russian for one. Although I have forgotten most of what I learned I would like to try to reconnect with those languages again. Or I can take a totally different course or courses in something I have never studied, for it doesn't cost anything for me to store the knowledge.

Since I feel I have almost fifty years of life left there is no reason why I can't do all of those and a lot more. There is so much for me to do that I wonder if, even with living to 120, I will have long enough to do them all.

* * *

I am not pleased to say that my thinking about elder people and on becoming a senior has not always been favourable. When I was a child the block of houses to the north of us seemed to be where old people lived. Our blocks were divided by an avenue and while I went to the south, the east, and the west of where I lived I don't ever remember crossing the avenue to the block to the north. I would stand on the corner, though, and look. There were tall trees along their street while ours had none and their houses were smaller. Maybe it was from reading about Hansel and Gretel, but their part of the street always seemed dark and creepy to me, while ours always seemed light and airy.

I would see the old people walking along the street going home from an outing or heading somewhere. For most of them my memory is hazy, a man who always wore a dark heavy suit, a man who smoked cigars, a woman who had few teeth. But there is one whose image has always stayed with me. She lived a few houses down from the corner and I would see her on the street or in her yard. She was overweight and stooped so that her dress hung down in front and up in the back and she had white hair. Her legs were lumpy and discoloured from varicose veins. Her name was Mrs. Paisley, and I don't know her age but with the association that goes on in a young mind, to me she was very old.

And she has been the personification of old age for me ever since, to the point that I have never bought any clothes with the paisley pattern, and I have been embarrassed to admit that I have varicose veins.

As people are growing up, what they learn from their parents, society, teachers, and the media is how they view the world around them. How easily I became prejudiced against older people, and this was reinforced for most of my adult life by what I saw around me. Those in charge of all the forms of media seem to control our perception of aging. Young people are on magazine covers, on television, in the movies. They symbolize power, health, and beauty. When we do see older people on television they are usually going senile or have some symbol of elder age such as a walker, or are in commercials showing them with aches and pains and needing a lot of drugs to get through their day. The media also uses words that stereotype older adults to the point where most people dislike, or look down on, or want to stay away from them.

And I believed all this until I began to approach my own elder years. But just as I was in awe about how good I felt at turning forty and fifty and sixty so I am thrilled to find that mentally and physically I am no different in my seventies. Now, from an older, and maybe wiser point of view, I can't understand my prejudice because I am still the same person I was when I was younger. So far even my body is the same. And I can imagine that the elderly people of my childhood felt the same. I guess it's a case of 'walk a mile in my shoes.'

There was a time in human history when elders were treated with as much respect as other members of society. In some cultures that is still true today but not in most developed countries. Older people have gradually been shunted into the background.

So, when and why did this happen? I wonder if it started with the setting of a retirement age. Did reaching the age of sixty-five suddenly mean a person was useless to the working community? Did Baby Boomers cause it by being more outspoken in our youth; by demanding more rights, ignoring the rules, and generally thinking we were entitled to more in life? Did our attitude that we knew more than our parents and grandparents cause an altering in our view of older people. Or did the transformation take place because of the two world wars, when men weren't accepted into the forces because of their age?

Or could the older people themselves have begun to believe they were of no use to society because they had a hard time understanding the rapid changes that have been taking place in our world over the past few centuries?

* * *

Ageism is a new word in my vocabulary. I looked it up in the dictionary and it is: discrimination against old or elder people.

Ageism encompasses words such as: dependent, ineffectual, decrepit, slow, feeble, senile, weak, and dotage, which are used to describe the prejudice against, and the categorizing of, elder citizens. Society thinks that an older person is not as valuable as a younger person.

The dictionary states that fatalism is the belief that fate controls everything that happens; acceptance of everything that happens because of this belief.

Fatalism is a term to show an elder person as accepting that deterioration must occur while aging because it has occurred in the past. And it is true that many people feel hopeless when they think of aging. They are too ready to resign themselves to the limitations that seem to take place as they grow older. Elder age for them means decline. That is because they have been misled to think that way, even by their doctors who use phrases like "at your age" or "for your age." These imply the aches and pains, the diseases, and the slowing down of the body that many older people experience are all natural and they should submit to them without a whimper.

Why did my friend's doctor say he would only live to his eighties? Is that because if he ate better and quit smoking, he'd live much longer? Or is it because the doctor had the mindset that eighty is as long as he or anyone is capable of living? Was the prediction the doctor's way of telling him he was going to live to his full life's potential as the doctor saw it?

In the dictionary the word efficacy is defined as: the power to produce the effect wanted; effectiveness.

This is the word I like. I believe that if we change that fatalistic attitude about what being a senior means, we will have efficacy and will produce the effect we want. As the saying goes, "The easiest way to change something is to change our own, and others, point of view of it."

We Baby Boomers have been a bulge in the population throughout our lives. When we were young we thought we could change the world for the better and maybe we did in some areas. There was a television show, called *The Monkees*, that I liked watching when I was in my teens. One line of their theme song went. *"We're the young generation and we've got something to say."* Well, now Baby Boomers are becoming the elder generation. I think we should modify the lyrics to: *"We're that same generation, and we've still got something to say."*

I think it would be wonderful if we Boomers could change today's accepted prejudices against older people, so we are thought to be just like everyone else. We have to get our attitude, our sense of entitlement back. We have to stop the belief that we are victims of aging and start showing the younger generations that growing older is not an unfortunate or unpleasant part of life; that it is a valuable time of life and elder people are to be appreciated. As we have set trends in the past, I believe Baby Boomers can set a new standard for the words "aging" and "older".

I am convinced that it is time to redefine the term middle age. I think we have the ability to take it to fifty, or sixty or seventy years of age because at seventy five, I consider myself to be in my middle years. If 150 is the age some scientists believe the human race can live to, I still have almost half of my life ahead of me.

Some organizations and stores have progressively lowered the age of those who they consider to be seniors from sixty-five to sixty to fifty-five and even fifty. That means my mother, at ninety-two, was a senior for up to forty-two years or almost half her life. Those who are centenarians have been seniors for half of their lives. When I reach the age of 120, I will have been considered, by society not by me, a senior for seventy years or 58% of my life.

Maybe it is also time to redefine elder age. Wouldn't it be exciting if it could be modified to begin at 100 years-of-age? My parent's generation began the longevity revolution. Many of them extended, and are extending, their elder years to their one hundreds and beyond. It is up to Baby Boomers to continue that but also take it to the next level. It is up to us to make it acceptable and even appealing to be older.

We can follow the example of Hollywood actress Mamie Van Doren, who at age seventy-two said. "I want to make it fashionable to be older."

* * *

I still have emotions as I age, the same emotions I had as a child and a young adult. I feel happiness and sadness and anger and love and disappointment like everyone else. Even now, I look forward to the Christmas season with all its lights and carols and presents under the tree. I wake up with eagerness on Christmas morning. And why not; I have the child I once was still in me, just like I have all the ages I have been inside me.

The year 2010 marked the sixty-fifth anniversary of the end of the Second World War. In 1946, the first of the Baby Boomers were born. In 2011, those same Baby

Boomers began to turn sixty-five and now each day thousands of North Americans reach that age.

We Baby Boomers began the free love movement of the 1960s and 1970s. We went to, or knew all about, the musical *Hair;* we brought human sexuality out into the open. But most of us cringe at the thought that our parents ever had sex, just as our children recoiled at the thought that we had sex. And most people are repulsed at the thought of senior citizens having sex.

Just as there is a stigma to being an older person, so there is a stigma to being an older person who is sexually active. Men are viewed as "old fools", "old goats", and even "dirty old men", while women are thought to be emotionally unbalanced or are just viewed as being unattractive and therefore sexless.

In their youth everyone looks for a man or woman who is appealing and shapely to mate with and have children. Attraction is an instinctive move in the reproduction game.

In our elder years reproduction is not the motive. For most, having sex is also about having companionship, having someone to touch, and being intimate with someone.

And it has nothing to do with outward appearance. Beauty, at all ages, is in the eye of the self-confident, warm, friendly, charming person that most people are. In elderly people it is not their looks that make them attractive. Their attractiveness comes from their experience, intelligence, achievements, and character. Wrinkles and gray hair have their own special beauty.

So, as a Baby Boomer woman, I have changed my attitude about myself and how I used to believe that my outside is what made me attractive. I have come to realize that the package is just wrapping. It's the inside that has the surprise. And I now must project that out to everyone I meet. In so doing I can change the attitude of those who view me.

Baby Boomer men could quit comparing their sexual prowess to their younger days. The sexual act does not always have to take place. Closeness, caring, and love are very important replacements.

When I was in my twenties I lived in a small community where everyone knew everyone else. One summer there was a huge scandal when a man and woman left their spouses and took off together. Part of what shocked everyone was that they were in their mid-sixties.

Speculation abounded as to why they would have done it. Surely, it was felt, they couldn't feel love. And certainly, they didn't do it for sex. So, what could be their reason?

It turns out that they had been having an affair and decided to leave. They were gone for about three months then returned home to their spouses who accepted them back. I never did find out the reason although rumour had it that they wanted some excitement in their lives.

So, loving and making love are a fact of life for the elderly. And why not? Everyone feels love and can be in love at every age. It is not an emotion that gets turned off when we reach a certain age.

Other animals age but don't realize what is happening to them. Humans are the only species that understands aging, yet we feel the need to sugar coat elder age with terms like "young at heart, forever young, eighty years young?" Why does that part of everyone's life have to be disguised? Are people embarrassed about aging? Do they think it is a disgrace to grow older? It is not as if anyone has a choice about aging. What everyone can do is decide how confidently and strongly they will age.

Today, many people try to thwart what they regard as aging by getting face lifts, dying their hair, and getting various types of implants. I have never thought about getting a face lift or any other surgical procedure in order to stay looking young. At first, it was because I had seen a face life operation on television many years ago and the thought of having my skin cut, pulled and prodded made me shiver. Now, I don't want one because my face represents who I am at my age right now, not who I was at thirty. Besides, no cosmetic intervention will change the fact that I am aging, and I will always age.

There is a huge volume of products offered to the public that are called anti-aging drugs or lotions. I smile because anti means preventing, counteracting, or being opposed to. Aging is something that cannot be prevented or counteracted. So, I think the word anti-aging could be called an oxymoron. People may be opposed to aging, but they can't stop it.

I now view my aging as another exciting time in my life. Like living my life to its fullest during all my years, I mustn't squander my elder years for any reason. I must continue to search, learn, and question. But I will do it within my own comfort zone.

Chapter 26
My Attitude and My Life Today

When my mother turned seventy, my niece asked her. "So, Grandma, do you feel any older?"

Mom answered. "I don't even feel old."

I believe one of the main differences between me aging well and me not aging well is going to be my attitude. My thoughts can have a huge effect on my mental and physical aging. If my life span has not been programmed into me at conception, then I can influence how and when I age. And I can certainly dictate how I think about my aging.

I have always been an upbeat type of person. I have a fun-loving, happy, look-on-the-bright-side, kind of outlook. I try to see the positive side to everything. My glass always has enough liquid in it for me.

My husband says that it doesn't take much to make me happy. And I agree. Getting a manuscript accepted for publication elates me. Taking a trip to another country excites me. Sitting by a flowing river relaxes me. Having my grandchildren visit delights me.

But it is the accumulation of the little things in my daily life that pleases me the most. Finding a used desk to give me more writing space, eating the first cherry of the season when I lived on an acreage on Vancouver Island, taking my dog for a walk through the bush, paying one dollar for a dozen canning jars at a secondhand store, or receiving a phone call from my children or grandchildren, are all the little things that make me happy.

A study has shown that people who are upbeat and satisfied with life may survive as much as twenty years longer than negative people. Positive attitudes boost the immune system. Confident-thinking people experience less pain, are happier, and have higher levels of energy. That is me.

Some elder people state they have become invisible members of society, that no one notices them at parties, in stores, or restaurants, or on the street. They feel that no one wants to talk to them or ask their opinion on anything because they have gray hair, or wrinkles. They feel like second class citizens.

I have thought about that and when I am out in public, there are people of all ages around me. I can't pay attention to each one of them. That doesn't make them invisible; it just means that I cannot notice everyone. My head would be swivelling constantly.

I really don't understand why some elderly people worry about it. They are giving those people too much control. They are letting them dictate how they feel about themselves. I believe it is my decision if I feel ignored and I can change that with my attitude. I can speak up, demand attention; I can go and do something different. I don't need to rely on anyone to validate me. I validate myself.

Right now, I don't particularly find any difference in how I am being treated in my seventies than I was in my thirties. But to avoid being ignored, I walk tall and look people in the eye. I speak up. I smile. I know, though, that someone else's point of view of me shouldn't carry more weight than my view of myself, that it doesn't matter what other people think of me. If I don't think of myself as a second class person then no one else can make me one.

If someone doesn't want to be with me because I am older then that is their loss. I am still as good a friend and person now as I have been at any other time in my life, and I will continue to be the same type of person until I die.

As I age further I will not accept the senior citizens' clothes that I find on the rack. I wonder who designs clothes for older women. Certainly not someone who thinks they have any fashion sense. I will wear what I like, what is suitable for my psychological age. What will stop me is embarrassing myself with clothes that are definitely not for my body type.

One saying I want to dispose of is "age appropriate." Just what does that mean? Who coined it? What defines age appropriate clothes, or hairdos, or actions? Why does age have anything to do with what I wear, or how I style my hair, or how I act? I think those should be decided by the individual person who wants to wear a certain outfit, or drive a certain vehicle, or have long gray hair, or take a holiday.

There were things I couldn't do when I was a child because they were dangerous or I was too small, or I didn't understand the consequences. When I became an adult I was trusted to make intelligent decisions about what I wanted to do and where I wanted to go. By the time I reach my elder years I will have been making decisions for myself for three-quarters of a century or more. If I am fit and healthy then there is no reason for me to be suddenly limited in what everyone else thinks I can "appropriately" do.

Another phrase I don't care for is "second childhood." Why, when an elder person tries something new or returns to an activity they used to do, is it termed "entering their second childhood?" Most people, when they are raising a family or working, do not have the time or money to pursue an activity they enjoy. They have to wait until later in life. I like to think of it as "everything in its time in my life."

When I tell people that I plan to live to 120 years-of-age they respond with "Why would you want to do that?" And their tone isn't inquisitive, it is more scornful and skeptical.

I respond. "Why would I want to die before my time? There is so much that I have not done in my life."

I have thought about dying as most people have. I know that death, whether I want to admit it or not, will end my aging. I have asked myself if I am afraid of death and sometimes the answer is yes, and at other times it is no. I am curious about what is on the other side.

Have I fixated on living to 120 to avoid dying? I really don't think so. Nor do I feel that trying to live to be 120 is a fruitless undertaking. Others are well on their way. People who have lived to be over one hundred have their own reasons for having attained that age.

Ruth Frith (Nee Pursehouse) of Australia, was the oldest active athlete who, when she died at the age of 104 on February 28, 2014, held many records in the World Masters Games. And those records still stand today. She is quoted as saying: *"Don't eat vegetables, because I never eat vegetables. I know people that like diets that will scream at me, (but) don't eat vegetables. I never have."*

When Clara Honeyman, a Surrey B.C. woman, celebrated her 105th birthday in

2007 she was interviewed for television. In her interview she kicked out her leg as she said. "I am 105 and still kicking."

She had a sense of humour and was proud that she had reached that age. She painted up until she developed arthritis in her hands, she liked to laugh, had a zest for life, and loved to play Bingo. Her mind was still sharp and when asked why she liked Bingo, she replied. "Because I win."

Her answer to the people who wanted to know the secret to her longevity was. "I tell them to mind their own business."

Clara died in 2008 at the age of 106.

While other people who have reached 100 years-of-age and over have not consciously worked at it, I am. I want to be as healthy when I reach the ages of eighty, and ninety, and 100, and even 120 as I am today. And why not? I'm as healthy today as I was at fifty, at forty, and at thirty. I'd even like to think I am as good as I was in high school, but I haven't stepped out onto a basketball court lately to test my theory.

If I persist with my conscious effort to live to be as old as I want, then it should happen. I use the words 'conscious effort' because I believe I can control my awareness of everything I do. It just takes desire and determination. It is up to me to make my life happen. I will not wait for it to happen because without my guidance, it won't. Now that I have decided to rule how my body ages, getting older holds lots of promise of new adventures for me.

In 2006, five women, who were 100 years of age or older, lived in a Rollo, USA, retirement community. They were Mildred Leaver (100), Grace Wolfson (100), Gladys Stuart (101), Mildred Harris (100), and Viola Semas (100). All of them agreed that it was years of doing work they loved that helped them live a long and happy life.

During an interview they all said many people would tell them that they didn't want to live that long. Mildred Leaver, who was still driving her own car, thought that it was sad, because as she put it. *"Aging is attitude and I don't feel old."*

At all stages in my life so far, I have had to go out into the world. The world and everything in it didn't come to me. I believe that my life is to be lived. I will not be a spectator of my own life. I will not vegetate physically or mentally. I will grow every day of my life.

At fifty-eight years of age, I joined a senior's dragon boat team as steersperson and took part in the B.C. Senior's Games. It was the first time dragon boating had been in the games and it was as a demonstration sport. Now, it has been incorporated into the games as a bona-fide sport.

That year I went with my breast cancer survivor team to a dragon boat festival in Australia. Since pink is the colour associated with breast cancer, the day before the festival there was a pink parade. All the twenty-two members of the fifty-eight teams dressed in some sort of pink clothes or costumes and we paraded through the streets of Caloundra, New South Wales, where the festival was held. The festival lasted two days and then most of my team and I toured through parts of Australia. Before heading home some of us visited Fiji for a week.

Also, during my fifties, I began writing fiction and trying to break into the fiction novel market. I had a short story published and then at fifty-nine my first mystery novel, *Illegally Dead*, came out. At sixty-one my second mystery novel, *The Only Shadow in the House* was published. I have had five more mysteries, five historical, two holiday romances, and two sci/fi novels published since then.

At sixty-one I took two of my grandchildren on a tree top adventure at the WildPlay Elements Park, near Nanaimo, B.C.. We climbed high in the trees, hooked ourselves to guide wires and manoeuvred our way over moving logs, and planks, and stirrups, fought our way across hanging cargo nets, zip lined, and generally spent two hours working our way along the ever increasingly difficult course. I have done that many times since with other grandchildren.

When I was sixty-five, my husband and I took a ten-week, round-trip, motorhome tour to Florida where I met up with my dragon boat team and we competed in another international breast cancer survivor dragon boat festival. My team flew down, but I decided I wanted to see the countryside between my home on the west coast and Florida on the east coast.

At sixty-seven I hiked part of the Juan de Fuca Marine Trail, west of Victoria, B.C., with two of my grandchildren. I also took part in two 5K inflatable races with my daughter and three grandchildren. At sixty-eight, I hiked 11km (7 mi) of the Appalachian Trail in Connecticut.

For seven years I walked/jogged in an annual 5K walk/run with two friends and I have done 5K and 10K walks with family members. At seventy years of age, I made it to the end of the 384 metre (1270 ft.) long Riverbend Cave (part of the Horne Lake Caves). To reach that end I had to repel down a 21 metre (70ft) rock wall.

In my seventies, I walk five kilometres three evenings a week and dragon boat two evenings in the summer. In the winter I toboggan with my great-granddaughter, walk half an hour when the weather permits and start indoor training for dragon boat season in February. Plus, I still do my own exercises of weightlifting, stretching, and Tai Chi.

There isn't anything I can't do at any age.

* * *

In the dictionary gerontology is explained as: the branch of science dealing with the phenomena and problems of aging and old age. When I looked up 'phenomenon' in the dictionary I found many different definitions. The two I like and that I now apply to my aging are: any exceptional fact or occurrence; something or someone extraordinary or remarkable.

I am taking part in another extraordinary occurrence in my life, just as I have in all my life's stages.

I don't think any different now than I have throughout all the ages of my life. I still like to have fun, be adventurous, try something new, and generally enjoy life. When I lived on Vancouver Island and my children and grandchildren came to visit in the summers, one of my favourite fun things to do was take them spelunking at Horne Lake caves. The first year I went there three times with visitors. The second year it was twice. These first explorations were short, more to find out how everyone liked being underground. Each year afterwards as my grandchildren grew older, I took them on tours further into the cave.

I am so looking forward to what changes my seventies and beyond will bring me. I know I plan on writing more books, and I want to travel more, but the rest is open for whatever I wish.

I am proud to be in my mid-seventies because I know that I have an advantage over the younger generations. I know that I have made it this far and fulfilled a lot of my dreams. They don't know if they will.

I think, because of that advantage, elder people should feel a bit of superiority to the rest of the population.

I, and only I, have control over my life and I will not accept that at a certain age I am on my way to death. I will not be dying mentally or physically for the last years of my life. I want to be living physically and mentally right up until the milli-second I die. I refuse to let ageism and fatalism apply to me. I will not let my chronological age decide what I am capable of doing. Efficacy, the power to produce the effect wanted, is the word I now live by.

I am not going to hope that I live to a fulfilled, older age. I am not going to hope that my mind and body keep performing at the same rate. I am not going to hope that I have a good life. I have turned the word `hope' into the word `action' and I am taking action to make sure all of those happen. I will endeavour to keep my mind and body active, and I will strive to live to a fulfilled older age.

According to the poem, *Desiderata*, I am a child of the universe; I have a right to be here—even when I am a senior citizen. And in order to change the way of thinking of young people I, as part of the next elder generation, have to start dispelling the myths about older age and start demanding respect right now.

So, I must show that the words that have become synonymous with aging such as frail, stooped, slow, decrepit, and senile can be replaced with the words active, healthy, alert, fun loving, adventurous, experienced. I want to purge the image of an old, worn out, lost person sitting in a senior's home. Because for the most part it is just an image.

Stats Canada says that only about 7% of elders are in nursing homes. Most live in their own homes into their eighties, nineties and beyond.

So comes the question: Does everyone want to live to one hundred years or older? That is another issue entirely and quite a personal one. Obviously, it is up to each individual to decide. Each person must come to terms with the fact that we do have a choice in how long and how well we live. And even if some don't want to live that long, they should still strive to have a healthy life to whatever age they reach. We must take total and complete advantage of our elder years. They are ours.

As a Baby Boomer I have the power to be an example of what a healthy and vigorous elder age is like. Therefore, I can't shuffle, I must walk; I can't slouch, I must stand tall; I can't allow my mental abilities to falter, I must remain sharp and spirited. And the best and easiest way for me to accomplish this is through the right diet, mental and physical exercise, and attitude.

I am not afraid of older age. I now refuse to accept the myths that my legs will slow down, that my memory and mind will fail, that I will develop a disease. I have changed the mental hold older age had over me for many of my younger years.

Many concepts that applied throughout my life will still apply in my elder years. If I can cope with any situation I can survive it. Therefore, I look at aging as the next act in my life's play, just like finding my first job, getting married, and raising children were new acts. I can and will adjust to the life ahead of me. Again, the choice is mine. It is within me to make it happen.

Aging: accept it; embrace it; run with it; have fun with it. For aging is a human right that is denied to many. Aging is mine to do with as I please.

* * *

I have learned so much about how to reach my goal of living to 120 years-of-age and how to be healthy while doing it to the point that I now have a love/hate relationship with food. I still love to eat it, but, knowing what some of it can do to my body, I hate it.

If it were a perfect world I would be able to state that no harmful foods have passed my lips in years. But I am not a saint and even with all the knowledge I have gained, it has been a slow change, because eating is my passion, and sweets and chocolate are still my downfall.

I have managed to reduce the amount of sugary foods I eat and replace them with more nutrient rich foods. Because of that I do have more energy and I am more alert. And by eliminating the foods that are high in sugars I have also excluded the many fat calories also found in them. For snacks, I eat popcorn and fruit.

I try to get vitamins and minerals from the food I eat but I also take them in the pill form.

I still like my peanut butter sandwiches but now I buy the natural peanut butter with no added sugar, salt, or hydrogenated vegetable oils. I asked a young boy I knew why he never put butter on his bread when he had a peanut butter sandwich. He answered. "Because I already have the butter in peanut butter." I haven't used margarine or butter on mine since then.

I strive to keep my food intake to 2000 or less calories on weekdays but relax a little on the weekends.

I am lenient when we go out for a meal or to friend's homes. I make a pact with myself. If I eat lots of vegetables and salad, then I can have dessert. I do try to stay away from fries and other deep fried foods.

When I am sitting at the computer and writing, to combat the urge to stuff myself with chocolates, I eat my meal then drink mugs of green tea to keep me feeling full for the morning or afternoon. That gives me my diversion without the calories. I do have one can of pop a day.

Even though I never really drank much alcohol, except at Christmas, I now only have a drink on special occasions.

I have substituted many healthy foods for the damaging ones. I have always liked vegetable salads, mashed carrots, and bean salads. I find multi-grain breads so much tastier than white bread. Oatmeal has made its way back into my life for breakfast. There are so many foods that I do savour that are good for me. Only now, I eat them more often.

I have tried to redirect my eating urges into something else that I want to do; something that I can remember and look back on with pride. Overindulging in a ten course meal to the point of sickness is not what I can look on with any sense of accomplishment. I don't remember that piece of pie, or cake, or chocolate bar I had to have but I do remember the painting I did, or the book I wrote, or the yard I landscaped.

I have found that the longer I eat healthy foods that are beneficial for my body, the better I feel mentally. Not so much because it is helping my mind but because I feel good about myself. I am doing something for me.

There are still times, though, when the eating habits of old have called to me and I have answered. I am sad to say that my good intentions sometimes become lost when my taste buds go into action. Since learning about food and my body, I find that when I do eat something unhealthy for my body, I feel mentally sick. I can almost picture the abuse it is wreaking on my body as it courses through my digestive system and into my blood stream and organs.

I finally understand that eating unhealthy foods gave me a boost when I needed to deal with what was happening in my life. I felt I was treating myself by eating all that was bad for me. I shudder at the fact that I was really punishing my body and I am thankful that my body has come through for me. So, every time I resist the urge to have junk food like a chocolate bar, chips, or cake, I congratulate myself on extending my life a little bit more.

I have changed my lifestyle so that in the future if something goes wrong with my health, I will not look back and think, "if only I had made a change when I had the chance." I will know that I did all I could to ensure my longevity.

I have also made changes in other areas of my life. I've developed more restraint in my driving as I grow older. I don't feel the need to get some place in a hurry. Whenever possible I pull over to let other vehicles pass me. I have figured out that being in a rush only gets me to my destination about five minutes faster than when I drive at normal speed. I value my life more than I value those five minutes, or to put it a better way, I am not in that much of a hurry to die.

I have learned to be cautious without being scared. I look around, I analyze. I realize my mind and body are fragile, that there are so many ways that I can be hurt both physically and mentally. I am more observant of the world around me. I look for potential problems and fix them. I try to visualize the outcome of something to know whether it is safe to try. I slow down and think. I don't go through life believing it will treat me better than other people. I know I am not invincible. I can be hurt or killed.

A cousin of mine was cleaning the snow from his roof when he slipped and fell off. He broke his back when he landed. He was confined to a wheelchair until his death. Another man I know leaned too far on a ladder, which slipped causing him to fall. He also broke his back and was in a wheelchair for the rest of his life. Two women friends of mine have had multiple operations on their knees, which had been giving them problems due to accidents.

I suppose I will stand a greater chance of living to the age of 120 if I stay in my house and never go anywhere. But that is not the type of life for me. I want to live a long, full, eventful life.

I seldom get headaches and when I do I know what causes them: I am tired, or I am hungry. All I do to correct the situation is rest or eat and the headache goes away. I don't have any aches or pains or any of the problems that are supposed to occur as we grow older.

Although I was raised in the 1960s, I did not do drugs. I never wanted to relinquish control of my mind, my thoughts, and my body to a drug. Today, I do not take medications of any sort, not even ASA, and I am not allergic to anything.

Will I remain here in Edmonton for the rest of my life? I don't know. I like change. Change keeps me alive. However, it is not where I live that is important to my life's plan. What matters is that I take my knowledge with me. I must always maintain my attitude, my exercise, and my good eating habits. Those I can do anywhere. Plus, I must continue to learn about my health by reading recently published books, by listening to health shows, and most importantly, by listening to my body. It will tell me if I am doing something wrong.

Will I reach 120 years-of-age with the changes I have made and are still making? Only the future will tell. What I do know will happen from me making these changes is that I will have a better life now and I have a purpose for each day of my future.

If I reach 120, great. If I don't then my consolation prize is that I will have given myself the best elder years possible. It's definitely a win/win situation for me.

I would like to think that I am starting my next forty-some years as healthy as I was at the beginning of my first seventy-some. However, I am not entering them as trusting or as innocent as I was when I was born.

If you enjoyed this journey, please leave the author a review.

Chapter 27
Living Proof

My goal in life is to live to my full life potential and I think my chances are very good. My genes are in my favour, and I ate well for most of my early, formative years. All the years of exercising have been good for my body and has certainly helped to counterbalance my bad eating habits so that my organs, systems, and bones are in exceptional shape. My diet is now much better, and my attitude is positive.

A centenarian is a person who has lived to be 100 years-of-age or more. They have lived that long because that was what their body was designed and destined to do. I now know what the design is for my body, and I am shaping its destiny through conscious effort.

CBC news stated that Canada's centenarian population was 11,500 in 2023, a three-fold increase from 2020.

Interviews of some centenarians show they have many character traits in common. They have been strong, resilient, and optimistic people all their lives and still are.

They have a sense of control, are more relaxed, adapt to changes, seldom get angry, and are emotionally stable. They don't indulge in self-pity.

Throughout their lives they have dealt with emergencies better than most people and they have coped quickly without much hostility or aggression. Getting their emotions back to normal and accepting everything as part of life have been two survival techniques they have used. They get their life on track again before physical and mental damage can be done, because that is one of the essentials to successful aging.

Women have a different personality than men and this could be why 80% of all centenarians are women and 75% of those are widowed. Most are living on their own, either alone or with the help of a family member or home care.

A super centenarian is someone who has lived for 110 years or longer and most of them are women. One in one thousand centenarians reach the super status but only 2% of them attain the age of 115 years or more. I want to be that one person. I want to put my name on the ever growing list of centenarians and then take it one step further and become a supercentenarian.

The Guinness Book of World Records has had a category for the oldest person in the world since 1955, which was usually filled by women. It began the separate classification of oldest man in the year 2000.

There have been more than 1000 documented super centenarians throughout history which is just a fraction of the ones who have actually lived to that age. The earliest super centenarian accepted by the Guinness Book of World Records is Thomas Peters who was born in Groningen, Netherlands, on April 6, 1745. He died on March 26, 1857, just shy of his 112th birthday.

Because of the United States' large population in the late 1800s, early 1900s, it has the highest number of centenarians today. Japan has the second highest number. The United Nations estimated that there are approximately 593,000 centenarians worldwide and women outnumber men by about four to one.

In order to be called a centenarian a person is required to have multiple, independent, documentary confirmations of their birth date. Neither the person, nor his or her family, are able to just make the claim and have it accepted. They need the necessary papers.

It has been hard to verify the dates of some of the centenarians because there haven't been compulsory birth records in many countries. Sweden has been keeping satisfactory records of births and deaths since 1750 with an improved system begun in 1850. France and Denmark had compulsory birth registration by the end of the nineteenth century. The United States began a universal birth record keeping in

1940. There were no written records in Russia before 1932.

Universal civil birth registration began in Quebec in 1679. Between the 1860's and 1880's it was initiated in other parts of what was to become Canada. Newfoundland, which joined Canada in 1949, set up its record system in 1892.

The churches in frontier Canada played a large role in keeping track of births, deaths, and marriages. Also, the census was begun in the late 1800s so it has been relatively easy to confirm the age of Canadian centenarians.

There are *domains of longevity* also known as *blue zones* in Japan, Italy, and Canada. The people on the island of Okinawa, Japan, have more centenarians per capita than any other place on earth. The population aged fifty and over is listed as a World Longevity Region because they still follow the original diet of vegetables, fish, and soy, and eat about 15% less calories than the rest of Japan. However, the residents on the island who are under fifty years of age do not fall into this category because they eat a western diet. Their health has suffered so much that their life expectancy is now lower than that of mainland Japan.

In eastern Sardinia, Italy, there is a founder population who are direct descendants of the original settlers of the island. There are about 13.5 centenarians per 100,000 residents in that group.

Nova Scotia, Canada, has a Longevity Belt where centenarians number fifty per 100,000 as opposed to twenty-one per 100,000 in the rest of Canada and eighteen per 100,000 in the United States. This Longevity Belt is situated between Yarmouth, settled by New Englanders, and the historic town of Lunenburg, settled by Germans. Both these towns were first established in the 17th century. Scientists are studying these people to see if there is a longevity gene since many of them are descendants of the original founders.

Obviously, longevity is not a new phenomenon. It has been happening for centuries. What is new is that I now know what can shorten my life and how to extend my life's potential. And it is just so simple: eat right, exercise, and have an upbeat attitude.

As one researcher put it. *"The older you are, the healthier you've been."*

Author's Last Words

It wasn't until I began to write this book that it dawned on me how much death there has been in my life and how many people I know have died before reaching sixty years of age, less than half their maximum life span.

Yet, older age, which used to be sixty, is now eighty, ninety or more. There have never been as many older citizens as there are today. The fastest growing segment of the population is centenarians, with the over eighty-five years-of-age group coming in second. Canada has 7.6 million residents who are sixty-five years and older and most of them are healthy and alert.

When I was young I looked upon aging as a terrible, unavoidable downward spiral into senility and illness. After reaching my forties and fifties with my body still working for me, I realized that I will always be me no matter what my age. I have found that the changes I had always perceived would take part in my body as I grew older are just that, perceived.

I won't necessarily have to walk stooped over because of osteoporosis. I won't necessarily lose my flexibility, endurance, or stamina. The afflictions like heart disease, joint problems, and muscle weakness (including the heart) that I have always thought were synonymous with aging are really caused by the cumulative effects of bad habits such as smoking, a high fat, low fibre diet, and lack of exercise. Most digestive problems, hardening of my arteries, dental disease, loss of muscle tone, and middle-age spread will not be brought on by my aging. I can dictate whether I will be affected by them at all.

Learning that I have control over my aging was a plus and it made me wonder if all these diseases are a normal part of aging OR do the people who don't develop these diseases represent normal aging? I'm opting for the latter, thinking that maybe they are not supposed to be typical of older age. They are diseases and, for the most part, can be avoided with simple lifestyle changes. After all, there are people in their thirties, forties, and fifties having heart attacks, strokes, and dying from cancer.

The twenty years between forty-five and sixty-five are the most difficult for many people to survive. That is when all the negative factors that are part of their lives, such as a sedentary lifestyle, alcoholism, elevated cholesterol, poor genes, harmful eating, and smoking, begin to show their effects. Two male friends of mine have been fighting prostate cancer since their fifties.

Another male friend had a kidney removed in his early sixties because of cancer.

Many of the books on shelves today are concerned with preventing aging. They cater to most people's desire to foil the aging clock. They stress how to stay young as if aging was a sin and should be avoided at all costs.

And advertisers would have consumers believe that looking young equates with staying young. However, getting Botox to remove facial wrinkles, or using the latest lotion and treatment on our faces, or having a facelift will not lengthen our lives. It may prevent the users from looking older, but it will not prevent them from getting older.

Since there is no such thing as anti-aging and denying that I will grow older is not my intention, I decided to write this book about my embrace of aging, and of my intent to be healthy and happy for my next forty-some years.

I have a lot of life experience and I am now putting that experience, combined with what I learned from all my research, into practice. I will make aging work for me. I will not spend time and energy on fighting it. Because I know nothing is going to stop it and nothing is going to slow it down. The minutes are ticking away for everyone. It is inevitable. I have admitted that and now I am free to get on with the rest of my life.

If I look at my life as living right up until I die, then I have years to fulfill all the dreams I've ever had. Just because I didn't accomplish a pre-determined plan by a certain age doesn't mean I am a failure. I have a long time yet to do it, because a failure is really someone who quits too soon. And I liberated myself from the mental cut off point I had set where I would be too old to learn or do anything new.

I've decided that time of my life should be called older age or elder age instead of old age. Old has a stationary sound to it, like I will have reached the end and cannot move forward anymore, while older denotes a sense of motion, activity. The word elder implies wisdom, experience, and respect, and gives that age the dignity it deserves.

The dictionary defines the word "keep" as: to have for a long time or forever; to have and not let go; retain under one's control; to have and take care of.

I have had my body for a long time; it is mine to have and not let go; its survival is under my control; and it is up to me to take care of it. So, this is what I must do.

Keep exercising both my body and my mind. I always want to know that my body will do anything I ask of it. If my mind says climb these stairs I want my body to be able to do it. I never want my mind or body to say the words "I can't." I want the mental and physical parts of me to act as one, to not be torn apart by mental or physical diseases.

Keep my body at its ideal weight. To me that is a weight I feel good at; the weight at which my body will perform all that I decide I want to do, whether it's hiking, dragon boating, or bicycling.

Keep my blood pressure within limits by exercising.

Keep my cholesterol low, my HDLs high, and my LDLs low.

Keep track of my blood sugar and insulin levels.

Keep my stress down.

Keep looking forward to each day.

Keep a good outlook and attitude.

Keep learning.

Keep working on eating better.

Keep enjoying and making changes to my life.

Keep wanting to live to 120 years-of-age.

And if I get to 120 years of age, I just might decide to live three more years and set a new record.

* * *

There is a website https://en.wikipedia.org/wiki/List_of_oldest_living_people with a list of fifty of the oldest centenarians and supercentenarians, all of whom are still alive. Many are longevity record holders for their country. This list is changing constantly as some pass and new names are added and it is not even close to the actual number of centenarians and supercentenarians there are in the world.

This is also a website listing the oldest living people in Canada: https://gerontology.fandom.com/wiki/List_of_oldest_living_people_in_Canada

Only one person, Jeanne Louise Calment, has been proven, through documentation, to have lived for over 120 years. Others have challenged that title but there was no documentation to support their claim. Here are a few who have come very close.

*Kane Tanaka of Japan was born on February 21st 1875 and died April 19th 2022. She lived for 119 years and 107 days and is the second oldest person ever next to Jeanne Calment. She is the oldest Japanese ever.

*Sarah Knauss of the United States was born on September 24, 1880 and died December 30, 1999 at the age of 119 years and 97 days. When she celebrated her 119th birthday her daughter was ninety-five-years-old, her grandson seventy-years-old, great-granddaughter almost fifty, great-great-granddaughter in her late twenties, and her great-great-great-grandson was four.

One of the reasons for Sarah's longevity could be explained by one of the staff at the home where she lived. *"Sarah has an attitude of live and let go. She has a real serenity. She's also very kind. She's very grateful."*

*Lucile Randon of France ranks as the fourth longest living person at 118 years and 340 days. She was born on February 11th, 1904 and died on January 17th, 2023. She was known as Sister Andre and also has the honour of being the oldest survivor of the Covid pandemic. She tested positive a month before turning 117.

*Lucy Hannah lived from July 16, 1875 to March 21, 1993. She was 117 years, 248 days old when she passed away. Lucy was the second oldest verified person to have ever lived in the United States and the world's fifth oldest person to have ever lived. She was never the world's oldest living person because Jeanne Calment was five months old when Lucy was born and Jeanne was still alive when Lucy died.

*Canadian Marie-Louise Meilleur was born on August 29, 1880, thirteen years after the confederation of Canada on July 1, 1867. She was 117 years, 230 days of age when she died on April 16, 1998. Marie-Louise had ten children and at the time of her death had eighty-five grandchildren, eighty great-grandchildren, fifty-seven great-great-grandchildren and four great-great-great-grandchildren.

Marie-Louise cited hard work as the reason for her longevity and she did enjoy a glass of wine. She also quit smoking at the age of 90.

*Misoa Okawa was born in 1898 in Japan and was the oldest person in the world from 2013 until her death in 2015 at the age of 117 years, 27 days. She believed that eating, sleeping and relaxing were the three keys to a long life. On her birthday when asked how she felt about the past 117 years she said. "It seemed rather short."

Of the oldest men, Shigechivo Izumi, of Japan, was said to be the oldest living man when he died in 1986 at 120 years 237 days of age. It was claimed that he was born in 1865. But that was unverified and has been disputed by some Japanese scholars who did additional research and believe that his birth date may have been confused with that of an older brother who died at a young age.

*Jiroemon Kimura became the oldest verified male on December 28, 2012 when he surpassed Danish-American, Christian Mortensen's age of 115 years, 252 days. He was the first undisputed man to reach 116 years of age. He died at the age of 116 years, 54 days on June 12, 2013.

*Christian Mortensen, born Thomas Peter Thorvald Kristian Ferdinand Mortensen, lived from August 16, 1882 to April 25, 1998. He emigrated from Denmark to the United States in 1903. Although, he was briefly married he had no children. He only smoked the occasional cigar. He was the first male to reach the age of 115 years.

*Puerto Rican, Emiliano Mercado del Toro, August 21, 1891 to January 24, 2007, was the world's oldest person for six weeks and the world's oldest man from November 19, 2004 until his death at age 115 years, 156 days.

The average time that a person has served as the oldest living person in the world is 525.5 days.

The End

The Art of Growing Older Bibliography

Books

Atkinson, Mary. *A Practical Guide to Self Massage*. Montreal: Reader's Digest Association, Inc., 2005

Austad, Steven, N. *Why We Age*. Toronto: John Wiley & Sons, 1997.

Beare, Sally. *50 Secrets Of The World's Longest Living People*. New York: Marlowe & Company, 2006.

Bortz, Walter, M. *We Live Too Short*. Toronto: Bantam Books, 1991.

Brantley, Dr. Timothy. *The Cure*. Hoboken: John Wiley & Sons, Inc, 2007.

Butler, Robert N. M.D. *The New Love and Sex After 60*. New York: Ballantine Books, 2002.

Callahan, Lisa. *The Fitness Factor*. Guilford Connecticut: The Lyons Press, 2002.

Challem, Jack. *Feed Your Genes Right*. Hoboken: John Wiley & Son, Inc.: 2005.

Consumer's Reports. *Guide to Diet, Health & Fitness*. New York: Shoreline Publishing Group LLC, 2005.

Chopra, Deepak. M.D. *Ageless Body, Timeless Mind*. New York: Random House. 1993

Chopra, Deepak. M.D. & Simon, David. M.D. *Grow Younger, Live Longer*. New York: Harmony Books, 2001.

Clark, William R. *A Means To An End*. New York: Oxford University Press. 1999.

Day, Trevor. *Genetics*. San Diego: Blackbirch Press. 2004

Edwards, Peggy, et al. *The Juggling Act*. Toronto: McClelland & Stewart Ltd. 2002.

Fisher, Patricia, Editor. *Age Erasers For Women*. Rodale Press, Inc. 1994.

Ford, Norman D. *Supercharge Your Immunity*. New Canaan: Keats Publishing, Inc., 1998.

Francina, Suza. *The New Yoga for Healthy Aging*. Deerfield Beach: Health Communications, Inc. 2007.

Fuhrman, Dr. Joel. *Eat for Life*. New York City: Harper Collins. 2020.

Goldberg, Dr. Bruce. *Look Younger, Live Longer*. St. Paul, Minnesota: Lewellyn Publications,1998.

Gundry, Dr. Steven. *The Plant Paradox*. New York City: Harper Wave. 2017.

Heinerman, John. *Anti-Aging Remedies*. Englewood Cliffs, New Jersey: Prentice Hall Inc, 1996.

Johnson, David. W. *Feel 30 For The Next 50 Years*. New York: Avon Books, 1998.

Kirkwood, Tom. *Time Of Our Lives*. NewYork: Oxford University Press, 1999.

Klatz, Ronald and Goldman, Robert. *Stopping the Clock*. New Canaan, Connecticut: Keats Publishing, Inc, 1996.

Kurzwell, Ray & Grossman, Terry. M.D. *Fantastic Voyage*. Rodale Inc. 2004.

Longo, Valter, *The Longevity Diet*. New York City: Avery, 2018.

McCord, Holly. *Win The Sugar War*. Rodale. 2002.

Medina, John, J. *The Clock of Ages*. Cambridge: Cambridge University Press, 1996.

Mindell Earl. *Earl Mindell's Anti-Aging Bible*. New York: Fireside, 1996.

Nulls, Gary. *Power Aging*. New York: New American Library, 2003.

Perricone, Nicholas, MD. *Ageless Face, Ageless Mind*. New York: Ballantine Books, 2007.

Pollack, Robert. *Signs of Life*. New York: Houghton Mifflin Company, 1994.

Ratey, John, J. M.D. *The User's Guide to the Brain*. New York: Pantheon Books, 2001

Reighman, Judith. M.D. *Slow Down Your Clock*. New York: Perennial Currents, 2004.

Roizen, Michael F. M.D. & La Puma, John. M.D. *The Real Age Diet* New York: Cliff Street Books. 1999.

Roizen, Michael F. M.D. & Oz, Mehmet C. M.D. *You, The Owner's Manual*. New York: HarperResource. 2005.

Sears, Barry. *The Anti-Aging Zone*. New York: Harper Collins, 1999.

Sellers, Ronnie. Editor. *60 Things To Do When You Turn 60*. Portland: Ronnie Sellers Productions, Inc., 2006.

Shealy, C. Norman. M.D., Ph.D. *Life Beyond 100*. New York: Penguin Group. 2005.

Small, Gary. M.D. *The Longevity Bible* New York: Hyperion. 2006.

Somers, Suzanne. *Ageless*. New York: Crown Publishers. 2006.

Somers, Suzanne. *Breakthrough*. New York: Crown Publishers. 2008.

Stille, Darlene R. *Genetics*. Minneapolis: Compass Point Books. 2006

Stoppard, Dr. Miriam. *defying age*. New York: DK Publishing, Inc, 2004

Ullis, Karlis,.and Ptacek, Greg. *Age Right*. New York: Simon & Schuster, 1999.

Ulrich, Karen. *How to Write Your Life Story*. Montreal: Reader's Digest Association, Inc., 2006

Wagorn, Yvonne et al. *Healthy Happy Aging*. Burnstown, Ontario: General Store Publishing house, Inc. 1991.

Walker, Richard. *Genes and DNA*. Boston: Kingfisher, 2003.

---------------- *Foods That Harm, Foods That Heal*. Montreal: Reader's Digest Association, Inc., 2004.

---------------- *30 Minutes a Day to a Healthy Heart*. Montreal: Reader's Digest Association, Inc., 2006.

--------------- *Extraordinary Uses for Ordinary Things*. Montreal: Reader's Digest Association, Inc., 2005.

Websites
Aspertame: https://pubmed.ncbi.nlm.nih.gov/7936222/

Antibiotic overuse: https://www.mayoclinic.org/healthy-lifestyle/consumer-health/in-depth/antibiotics/art-20045720

Brain aging: https://www.nia.nih.gov/health/brain-health/how-aging-brain-affects-thinking

Brain health: https://www.nia.nih.gov/health/brain-health/cognitive-health-and-older-adults

Calorie Restricted Diet: https://www.nia.nih.gov/news/calorie-restriction-and-fasting-diets-what-do-we-know

Centenarians in Canada: https://www.cbc.ca/news/canada/british-columbia/canada-centenarians-fastest-growing-1.7246790

Chemicals and kidneys: https://www.chemscape.com/resources/chemical-management/health-effects/kidney-damage

Corn syrup: https://www.healthline.com/nutrition/why-high-fructose-corn-syrup-is-bad

Coronary artery bypass surgery: https://www.hopkinsmedicine.org/health/treatment-tests-and-therapies/coronary-artery-bypass-graft-surgery

Deaths from smoking: https://www.healthdata.org/news-events/newsroom/news-releases/lancet-lancet-public-health-latest-global-data-finds-nearly-8

Deaths from pollution: https://www.hsph.harvard.edu/c-change/news/fossil-fuel-air-pollution-responsible-for-1-in-5-deaths-worldwide/

Decline in Life Expectancy: https://www150.statcan.gc.ca/n1/daily-quotidien/231127/dq231127b-eng.htm

Genetics and Aging: https://mcpress.mayoclinic.org/healthy-aging/how-much-do-genetics-influence-the-aging-process/

Graveyard shifts and cancer: https://www.hrreporter.com/focus-areas/safety/night-shift-a-probable-carcinogen-who/317010

Heart disease: https://abcnews.go.com/Health/story?id=118124&page=1

Heart Disease in Teenagers: https://abcnews.go.com/Health/story?id=118124&page=1

Heart Disease in Teenagers: https://abcnews.go.com/Health/HeartDiseaseRisks/heavy-kids-teens-heart-risks/story?id=12248667

Heart Disease in Teenagers: https://www.mountelizabeth.com.sg/health-plus/article/teenagers-and-heart-disease

Heart Disease in Teenagers: https://futurism.com/neoscope/doctor-warns-teens-already-clogging-arteries

Hormone Replacement: https://www.mayoclinic.org/diseases-conditions/menopause/in-depth/hormone-therapy/art-20046372

Hospital medical errors: https://nationalpost.com/feature/hospital-secrets-the-deadly-mistakes-they-keep-making

Human Growth Hormone: https://www.mayoclinic.org/healthy-lifestyle/healthy-aging/in-depth/growth-hormone/art-20045735

Karoshi: https://www.bbc.com/worklife/article/20210518-how-overwork-is-literally-killing-us

Personality traits of centenarians: https://www.newscientist.com/article/mg26034664-300-eight-personality-traits-may-help-people-live-to-100-and-beyond/

Phosphorus: https://www.healthline.com/health/food-nutrition/is-phosphoric-acid-bad-for-me#Potential-dangers

Phosphorus: https://www.ncbi.nlm.nih.gov/pmc/articles/PMC5693714/

Sedentary behaviour: https://www150.statcan.gc.ca/n1/pub/82-003-x/2020009/article/00002-eng.htm

Sense of Smell: https://www.ncbi.nlm.nih.gov/pmc/articles/PMC6381007/

Sleep and Health: https://health.gov/myhealthfinder/healthy-living/mental-health-and-relationships/get-enough-sleep

Sucralose: https://health.clevelandclinic.org/is-sucralose-splenda-bad-for-you

Sugar Substitutes: https://www.canada.ca/en/health-canada/services/food-nutrition/food-safety/food-additives/sugar-substitutes.html

Super Centenarians in Canada: https://en.wikipedia.org/wiki/List_of_Canadian_supercentenarians

Telemores: https://www.medicalnewstoday.com/articles/are-telomeres-really-the-key-to-living-longer-youthful-lives#Telomeres-and-biological-age

The Science of our Senses: https://medschool.vanderbilt.edu/vanderbilt-medicine/the-science-of-our-senses/

Theories on Aging: https://www.physio-pedia.com/Theories_of_Ageing

Unpaid caregivers: https://www150.statcan.gc.ca/n1/pub/11-008-x/2004002/article/7002-eng.pdf

Joan Donaldson-Yarmey was born in New Westminster, B.C., Canada, and raised in Edmonton, Alberta. Over the years she worked as a bartender, hotel maid, cashier, bank teller, bookkeeper, printing press operator, meat wrapper, gold prospector, warehouse shipper, house renovator, and nursing attendant. During that time she raised her two children and helped raise her three step-children.

Since she loves change, Joan has moved over thirty times in her life, living on acreages and farms and in small towns and cities throughout Alberta and B.C. She now lives in Edmonton with her husband and one cat.

Joan began her writing career with a short story, progressed to travel and historical articles, and then on to travel books. She called these books her "Backroads" series and in the seven of them she described what there is to see and do along the back roads of British Columbia, Alberta, the Yukon, and Alaska. She has now switched to fiction writing and is proud to be one of Books We Love Ltd published authors.

Sleuthing the Klondike, Rushing the Klondike, and *Romancing the Klondike* are Joan's Yukon Historical Novels, and *West to the Bay,* and *West to Grande Portage* are Joan's two Canadian Historical novels for adults and young adults.

She has had three mystery novels, *Illegally Dead, The Only Shadow in the House,* and *Whistler's Murder* published in what she calls the "Travelling Detective Series". They come in a boxed set. In her stand-alone novel, *Gold Fever,* she combines mystery with a little romance. *The Twelve Dates of Christmas* and *Single Bells* are a holiday romances.

https://www.bookswelove.com/donaldson-yarmey-joan/

http://thetravellingdetectiveseries.blogspot.com/

https://www.facebook.com/writingsbyJoan

Joan Donaldson-Yarmey's books published by BWL Publishing Inc.

Canadian Historical for Adults and Young Adults
Sleuthing the Klondike
Rushing the Klondike
Romancing the Klondike
West to Grande Portage
West to the Bay

Mysteries
Sleuthing the Klondike
Gold Fever
The Travelling Detective Series

Holiday Romance

Joan Donaldson-Yarmey and Gwen Donaldson
The Twelve Dates of Christmas
Single Bells

www.ingramcontent.com/pod-product-compliance
Lightning Source LLC
Chambersburg PA
CBHW051418290426
44109CB00016B/1352